"A pioneering family adventur
and joie de vivre, all bound to̞
on board and the incredible life Janis and Michel created. Their two
boys wonder, grow and thrive, from tiny passengers to crewmates
who become captain-worthy when life-threatening surgery sidelines
Michel for a time. Throughout it all, their steadfast and beloved
Cowabunga carries them ever forward, at times through seemingly
impossible situations. 'We were able to wrap the world around us,'
writes Janis, imparting a touch of the magic that seemed to guide and
watch over them. What a gift it is to sail along and catch the Cowabunga spirit!"

——Peter Stein, children's author of *Cars Galore* and the *Galore Series* at
Candlewick Press, and *Little Red's Riding 'Hood* of Scholastic Inc.'s
Orchard Books

http://painted-words.com/portfolio/peter-stein/
https://www.publishersweekly.com/pw/authorpage/peter-stein.html
http://www.smartbooksforsmartkids.com/tag/peter-stein/

"What a wonderful way to be a family: A must read. It's not just a
good story, I know those two boys who spent 10 years at sea with
their parents, and they both grew up to be good human beings who
care and make a difference every day!"

——Philippe Kahn, Inventor of the camera phone, *Time Magazine's*
2016 list of most influential images of all time, Owner/Helmsman of
the sailing team "Pegasus," CEO Fullpower Technologies

"Janis and Michel took their newborn and three-year-old sons on a
10-year 'boat schooling' experience. In this book, I discovered how
homeschooling two children at sea from France to California opened
this family to realities that cannot be learned on land."

——Delphine Duler, teaching professional at
Lycée Français de San Francisco

"Janis Couvreux has written a vivid and fascinating account of her
family's extraordinary journey. *Sail Cowabunga!* is a story of perseverance and determination, a story about personal growth and

relationships. Armchair travelers and adventurous types, this remarkable story is for you."

—Marlene Cullen, founder of Writers Forum of
Petaluma and host of The Write Spot Blog
www.TheWriteSpot.us

"Courageous and inspiring, *Sail Cowabunga!* is beautifully written, honest and rife with cruiser-moxie. This heroic story is a must-read for anyone considering a jump out of suburbia and into a quality life, rich with travel and adventure. Janis Lasky Couvreux's intriguing memoir is a culmination of her adventurous spirit, profound relationships, and on-the-water plights—all while navigating family life. *Sail Cowabunga!* is a seafarer's guide to living one's dreams; aptly exposing the equally imperative values of patience *and* perseverance."

—Lynne Rey, author of travel-school cruising blog
www.mvcortado.com

"One word describes this book, 'Magnifique!' This is a story of resiliency, teamwork, family, love and courage. As a landlubber, I was fascinated with life at sea for a young family. I know now why your fabulous son is so family oriented and adventurous. Cowabunga has new meaning for me."

—Keith Schneider, Assistant Chief,
West Metro Fire Rescue in Littleton, Colorado

"Sure, we have all engaged in a risky caper at some point. Yet, when do we hear of an entire family embarking upon an extended and unlikely adventure as this? Logistical conundrums from the simplest daily tasks, bureaucratic and mechanical complications, coping strategies to survive emergencies, all required exceptional physical and emotional stamina and resourcefulness. Try raising well-adjusted boys and keeping a marriage nicely afloat...on a boat. The Couvreux Family reinvented family traditions, found generous camaraderie at each port, and gazed toward the next horizon. This astonishing journey is full of surprises, and heart, to the very last."

—Laurie Lubeck, Editor, Japan Association of
Travel Agents Ecotourism Handbook

"The curious and courageous Couvreuxs and their trusty sail boat Cowabunga. Janis Couvreux, husband, Michel, and their two young sons invite the reader to squeeze into that sailboat as they ride the waves to places most of us will never venture: the complicated ports of Africa, strange islands smack in the middle of the Atlantic Ocean, tiny inlets along the eastern coast of South America, to name a few. Janis's exquisite storytelling style puts the reader in the thick of the adventure, from being rescued by the U.S. Navy to being the rescuers during a devastating flood in Brazil along with how to cook family dinner every night strapped into the galley, so the waves don't knock you over while you are stirring the soup. The life the Couvreuxs chose to live and the lives of others they got to share it with, even for a little while, paint a portrait of what it means to be human in its many varied forms around the planet. And because Janis has gifted us this book, *Sail Cowabunga! A Family's Ten Years at Sea,* the rest of us get to live it too. Cowabunga!"

—Elaine S. Silver, editor and writer

"What a delightful read. Janis's story has plenty of excitement without the drama and is a solid story of a family of adventurers. Sean (aka Doogie) is a great shipmate, and after reading this, I understand how he got to be that way.
—Dawn Riley, professional skipper, four America's Cup Teams, two Around the World Races, Youngest Sailor, and CEO of an America's Cup Team

SAIL
Cowabunga!
A FAMILY'S TEN YEARS AT SEA

Janis Lasky Couvreux

FILLES VERTES PUBLISHING

COEUR D'ALENE, ID

Filles Vertes Publishing, LLC
PO Box 1075
Coeur d'Alene, ID 83816
www.website-url.com

Publisher's Note: Although every precaution has been taken to verify the accuracy of the information contained herein, the author and publisher assume no responsibility for any errors or omissions. No liability is assumed for damages that may result from the use of information contained within. Some names and identifying details may have been changed to protect the privacy of individuals.

Book Layout © 2017 Filles Vertes Publishing
Cover Design © 2017 Broken Arrow Designs
www.brokenarrowdesigns.org

Books may be purchased in quantity and/or special sales by contacting the publisher.

Sail Cowabunga!/ Janis Couvreux. -- 1st ed.
ISBN 978-1-946802-04-0
eBook ISBN 978-1-946802-05-7

To the lives of my loves, Michel, Sean, Brendan and my grand-children Claire, Sky, Matthew, and Tao.

This is your story.

MESSAGE IN A BOTTLE

I had a minor catastrophe in my kitchen the other day. My beloved kitchen tongs broke, and I cried. I was heartbroken. Really? Yes, really. This couldn't be! I had used these nondescript, 30-year-old, Ace Hardware-type tongs daily for 10 years on our sailboat, Cowabunga, and for over 25 years since. They couldn't give up the ghost now.

These were the same tongs that had grappled with the 30 lobsters we caught on my thirtieth birthday in the middle of the Atlantic Ocean. These same tongs had plucked the Uruguayan snails from the bucket to become escargots. I had used them to retrieve steamy hot items from my oven, stove, and pressure cooker, and they were the ones Michel had always called for when flipping the meat on the grill at the back of the boat. These were the same tongs that our boys, Sean and Brendan, used to dig out their Lego pieces which were hiding under the floorboards. These treasured tongs had borne witness to our everyday life on the boat and so much more —and they broke! When it happened, Michel and I looked at each other. The end of an era? All that history up in smoke, poof! Just like that? So much emotion for a pair of cheap (and I mean really cheap) kitchen tongs.

No, this story wasn't going to end like this. Michel was determined that these tongs could be fixed to see another day. He had repaired them once before, replacing the rusted hinge screw that had succumbed to one too many saltwater dish washings. We both scoured the local hardware stores and came up with a replacement spring for the broken one, and it lived anew! I'm quite certain it will outlive us yet, and my family can be sure that some lucky soul will be inheriting this storied item in my will—our message in a bottle.

Petaluma, California, 2016

CONTENTS

ßEFORE THE ᏄAST

We were held captive by the currents of the Strait of Gibraltar. Like a hamster spinning in its caged wheel, we were trapped, baffled, and not making any headway on the water. The Strait was infamous for these quick-changing and strong conditions—a phenomenon caused by its funnel-like geographical configuration. We had a decent wind, but our efforts were to no avail. Frustrated, we gave up at the end of the day after a good eight hours of basically treading water. Our refuge for the night was in the Spanish enclave port of Ceuta, across the water from the Port of Gibraltar which we were trying to leave. At least we had the illusion of having made progress, spending the night in a different place. The next morning brought success. We carefully gauged the changing currents as prescribed by our nautical book's precise instructions, and the Strait spat us out.

It was October 1982, and we were two months into our new life of sailing and living on a boat as a young family of four. We had sailed from our home port in Le Verdon, France, in August of that year, intending to travel until either the money ran out or something forced us to stop. When friends introduced us to friends, they often introduce us as the ones "who sailed around the world." While we have friends from that time in our life who did just that, we didn't. We lived on *Cowabunga* for ten years, and it took us eight of those years to sail from France to California.

Before we began to sail, before I stood under the mast, and well before I had a husband or children, I had the itch to experience the world. My father told (and retold with age) unforgettable tales at the dinner table to my mom, younger brother, sister, and me. He spun stories of his experiences as a student in Switzerland and an ex-GI after WWII. His tales struck something deep within me, and I knew a seed of adventure had been planted. That's how it all started, and that's how I met my French husband, Michel, when I was a college student in France.

I desperately wanted to learn a foreign language with which I could ply a trade as a journalist. I was going to be *Time* magazine's next star foreign correspondent. I took advantage of the University of California at Berkeley's European Abroad Program (EAP) and began a year at the University of Bordeaux, France in the fall of 1974. Despite two years of college French, I was woefully inept at the language, and I felt terribly out of place my first several months in the country. Today, I realize that it was an excellent proving ground, daring me to move forward and conquer the unknown.

This is where my life veered from the blueprint I had set for my future. I met my kindred spirit and soul mate shortly after arriving in Bordeaux, which upset the whole apple cart. It didn't take long before I vacated the room I had rented in Bordeaux and moved in with him. He was in his last year at the School of Architecture, poised to pass his license exams. Michel was also an adventurous soul and shared my thirst for travel. Well before I met him, he had crisscrossed the entire United States by hitchhiking, from east to west, and north to south.

When we met on campus, he had just returned from an internship with an architectural firm in Visalia, California.

After we had both finished school, we married in Newport Beach, California, and then settled in the Medoc wine region near Bordeaux for the next seven years. Michel established his own architecture office, and during this time a friend invited us on his boat to sail to Spain. It was an epiphanic moment for us, seduced by starting in one land and waking up in another. We were thrilled to have alighted in a new place through the magic of sailing. It was the hallmark event that changed our lives, in which we decided to pursue our deep desire to travel, seeking adventure via a sailboat.

We wanted to start a family eventually, but we didn't want our children to grow up in suburbia with the idea that the world stopped at their door. They could learn so much more through travel; the world would be their teacher. Thus, we decided to "retire" with our young ones for as long as we could while they were young and impressionable. Traveling on a sailboat seemed to be an ideal method of travel while raising kids and spending vital time with them in their early years. We had a vision and began planning for our ultimate goal of sailing around the world.

We found *Cowabunga* when we weren't looking. She practically fell into our laps. Michel met a sailor and mentioned to him off the cuff that we had the vague idea of maybe buying a boat. This person just happened to have a vessel we may be interested in.

Cowabunga was a sleek, forty-two-foot Rorqual "ketch" (or two-masted), built in France in 1968. It was a cold-molded wood boat, which means thin strips of wood planks were laminated together diagonally for several layers, creating a sturdy and watertight vessel. But for us, *Cowabunga* wasn't just a boat. She became our ticket, our liberty, our way of living, our identity, our survival. She changed our lives dramatically over those ten years.

"Cowabunga" was originally attributed to a character in a 1950s children's TV show. It is now commonly accepted as an exclamation of pure joy, or a yell of exhilaration. Surfers are said to have adopted the phrase in the 1960s to punctuate their delight and enthusiasm when catching the perfect wave. When I first met Michel, he enjoyed surfing. Although I'm not sure if he knew that word at the time, with his then-limited English, he was familiar with the surfing culture and eagerly adopted the idea. We couldn't think of a more perfect name than *Cowabunga* to christen our future home with, and to represent our absolute excitement when we found her. The name embodied our cry of joy and would come to signify our passion for travel, discovery, and adventure. She would not only be our home, she would be the vehicle for our new life and our passport to adventure. Then before we knew it, she became our identity. On the seas, among other cruisers and families like us, we were known as the Famille Cowabunga—the Cowabunga Family.

We moved on board in the summer as a trial run when our first child was only a year old. The experience went so well that we decided to stay on through the winter. We never moved back to land, and officially set sail from our home port of Le Verdon, France in 1982 with our two boys, Sean and Brendan, then three years and five months old. We didn't have unlimited funds, so we started out with a "we'll just see how far and how long we can go" mentality. We would stop on occasion and work when the opportunity arose. It wasn't always perfect, nor always a wonderful life in paradise. It was a lot of effort— lessons in survival a good portion of the time. But one year led into another, and before we knew it, it had been ten years.

We enjoyed the snug, homey confines of *Cowabunga*, and the exhilaration of conquering the challenges of propelling oneself with (or against) the elements of nature. Events happened along the way that changed our goals, our expectations, our reality. We were forced to learn how to "go with the flow" when our plans didn't always mesh with what life dealt us. No, we didn't make it around the world, but we were able to wrap the world around us.

PART ONE

Europe

CHAPTER ONE

HOME IN FRANCE

It was 3 p.m. on a warm August afternoon in 1982 when we literally and metaphorically cast off the ties that bound us, slipping out to sea across the Bay of Biscay—the Golfe de Gascogne—in France, never to look back. We were jubilant and hopeful about the prospect of taking on new unknown adventures, but we were also nervous. This was our new life. But by creating a new normal of our own design, would we be doing the right thing by our children?

I had lived in France for seven years at that point. My life had already considerably changed from my Southern Californian, American middle-class, suburban upbringing. Born in 1954, I was part of the post-war baby boom and the new prosperity of the rising middle class. My father was a WWII veteran and the first in his family to earn a college degree, having grown up in the Depression Era. My parents met at Northrop Corporation in Los Angeles. My mother was a secretary, and my father was going places as a project and contracts manager in the early "go-go" days of a burgeoning aerospace industry that would soon give birth to manned space flight.

Young couples were able to easily purchase homes and cars then, and my parents established their tidy cocoon in Orange County, just south of Los Angeles. They were moving up in this new society: sun-bathed new neighborhoods, kids on new bicycles riding along the new sidewalks, new shopping centers, country clubs, and lawns hewn from tumbleweed-dotted empty lots. It seemed as though it could all have been a part of Disneyland, which, by the way, was only a few miles down the road in Anaheim, and also very new.

The turbulent 60s burst upon my high school scene, but they didn't chafe me too much. I was affected more heavily by my college experiences in the 1970s at the University of California at Berkeley, the seat of the "free speech movement" and anti-Vietnam war demonstrations. Somewhere along the line, I discovered that a life in suburbia didn't figure in my future plans anymore.

I liked the idea of backpacking around Europe, as was the fad in those years, but I had no idea how to prepare or organize such a trip. Since I was determined to learn to speak French fluently, spending a school year abroad seemed like an easier way to undertake a European trip while staying within the structure of a school year. I wouldn't fall behind in credits, and that would be my safety net.

Meeting a Frenchman, marrying, and living in France right out of college definitely helped me off the suburban track from the get-go. Michel and I lived in the Medoc wine region of Bordeaux, on the coast of the Atlantic Ocean. We were immersed in the aristocratic wine and food culture of this storied area. Here, Michel garnered architectural contracts with some of the chateaux (wineries), and I began a tentative journalism career in the Bordeaux wine public relations arena. While we were thrilled with our European situation as a new couple, we still craved more. We mulled over many ideas, but eventually, we were introduced to the one solution that would become our unconventional and wonderfully adventurous future.

One summer a friend invited us to go on with him on a sailboat for a small trip. We would go from the port of Arcachon, France, across the Bay of Biscay to San Sebastián, Spain. Oh my word! Such an eye opener that trip turned out to be. It was the hallmark event that inspired us—a seismic, monumental experience. It was our first experience boating at sea for multiple days, and after two nights, we had overcome (at least it seemed to us) some formidable elements to get from point A to point B. First, we successfully skirted breaking waves on a sandbar that bordered the channel passage out to the ocean, and Michel unfortunately lost his glasses overboard. Our second night was punctuated by some heady winds and agitated seas; we felt as if we'd really survived something.

We were equally seduced by the magic of starting in one country and waking up in another, having arrived under our own power harnessed from nature. We each had to take our turns standing watch at night—also a new experience. To make it even sweeter, neither Michel nor I got seasick. It was sunrise on the third morning of that trip, while we were savoring our coffee that we promised each other we would buy a sailboat and travel. To this day, over 40 years later, we can both turn to each other and note the time and date that we made that promise.

We were rather sure we wouldn't always live in France, but we didn't have any immediate plans on where we would go or how, until then. Having come under the spell of sailing, the only thing we knew for certain was that we had found the perfect solution to accomplish our dream of traveling as a family. Now we could start to plan for children!

I became pregnant with Sean, our first child, and Michel began fine tuning his sailing skills. He took some weekend sailing courses and participated in outings on the Gironde River through an accredited sailing organization. Aside from that week at sea from France to Spain, both of us only had minimal sailing experience dating back to our high school days. While we planned and learned, we also discovered that deciding to buy a boat, finding one, and affording one are all different things.

It was during one of Michel's sailing lessons that he met a man with a forty-two-foot ketch for sale in Port Grimaud, on the French Riviera. The size and description seemed to fit what we would be looking for, and possibly the price. Seizing the opportunity for a road trip, we took a few days and drove to the Cote d'Azur to check out the boat. Recognizing that we were novices and not really savvy on what constituted a viable one, Michel had contacted a boat appraiser and expert to meet us at the dock to render his professional opinion of the value, quality, and sturdiness of the vessel. While the boat needed a lot of TLC and would have to undergo substantial interior renovation to fit the lifestyle we envisioned, the hull and structure of the boat were deemed solid and in good shape by the expert, and well worth the asking price.

Michel thrived at the architectural firm he owned, and several lucrative jobs had come along about this time. Consequently, we were able to purchase the boat due to the anticipation of several promising projects. Getting the boat back to Bordeaux proved to be a separate hurdle. There were really only two options: sailing it back via the Mediterranean, past Gibraltar and to the port of Le Verdon, very near the Medoc wine region where we lived; or the more direct inland route, through the Canal du Midi by way of Toulouse and eventually Bordeaux itself. Since it was winter and we were short on time, we opted for the Canal route, which was not as easy as we projected.

Cowabunga, as we had already decided to name her, had a rather deep draft with a six-foot keel. The keel is a large, weighted, fin-like structure underneath the boat, which stabilizes the vessel and keeps it in balance, avoiding a capsize (thus the expression to be "on an even keel"). Due to our particularly long keel, the Canal wasn't quite deep enough in some places to accommodate us. Consequently, the boat scraped along in the narrower places but was able to make it through. Michel cobbled together a relay team of friends who helped us deliver the boat back in stages—weekends and short vacations—since neither no one was available to do the job in a single trip. A new team picked up *Cowabunga* where the last team left her along the canal, making headway in short spurts.

Starting from Port Grimaud, a team sailed *Cowabunga* east along the Mediterranean coast as far as the port of Agde, an entry-point for the Canal du Midi. Here, the masts were taken down and lashed lengthwise to the deck for the remainder of the canal trip since the boat couldn't fit under bridges fully rigged. For the next two weeks, the relay crew glided along postcard-worthy, serene, pastoral landscapes. Soft, grassy berms lined the waterways framed by arched, foliage-laden trees worthy of Monet's canvases. Our new home passed through such noteworthy places as the medieval fortified city of Carcassonne, and the Ville Rose (the "Pink City") of Toulouse—so named for its unique terracotta brick architecture. Our relay crews also enjoyed some incongruous moments like gliding in a viaduct suspended high above the Garonne river.

I didn't participate in this phase, being pregnant and not willing to face the rudimentary living conditions on board that existed at that early stage. Michel participated in as many of the relay stages as he could, and kept in constant contact with the current crew as to her daily whereabouts. He was onboard for the final stage, guiding *Cowabunga* to her new home with the onset of winter in 1978. I was elated as I spied *Cowabunga* rounding the final harbor breakwater and nearly gave out a cry of joy, just like her name implies. She was docked there for three years as we diligently set to scraping, painting, hammering, and transforming her.

For our first phase of renovation, we hauled the boat out of the water for some major work on the hull. It needed to be completely stripped down to the bare wood, refinished, and have new anti-fouling paint applied below the waterline. The two wooden masts were taken down as well and stripped of all the rigging for a new paint job. The stanchions (the upright deck perimeter support poles) and all other hardware on the deck were completely removed, thoroughly inspected, kept, or replaced with custom items. Michel gutted the inside, exposing the original structure and framing, rendering it a bare slate to reconfigure.

I wasn't much help at this early stage, becoming more ungainly by the day as my pregnancy with Sean progressed. I assisted in scraping off as much of the old exterior paint as I could from the least acrobatic position possible, which was simply standing. Michel transformed into a shipyard worker on weekends, holidays, and occasionally an abbreviated workday. The project overtook our budget, our birthday and Christmas lists, our dreams, our conversations. It was omnipresent in our lives. We even had wonderful friends come out of the woodwork to help us during these busy months so that we could meet our "first stage" goal of having the boat in the water by summer.

Michou, our local fisherman friend, often dropped by after an all-night fishing trip to extend a hand. He also lent tools and supplied us with buckets of fish and crabs for sustenance. Joel, a plumber whom Michel often employed on his construction sites, became a fast friend as well. He often dropped by the wharf with plumbing materials and strong-armed wrenching techniques. Then Philippe, who would become a very close friend of Michel's, also assisted when he could. But most importantly, he was perhaps the only other person besides me who understood Michel's passion for this adventure. He gave us his treasured 19th century antique barograph as a gift, and it held an honored place inside *Cowabunga* for the 10 years it was our home. Today that same barograph continues to give us the daily weather in our land-locked living room, 30 years after our departure. It also serves as a daily memorial to our friendship with Phillipe, since his passing several years ago.

Amidst all this, we had our first baby, Sean, in April of 1979. From day one, he was surrounded by and incorporated into our project. I would visit the job site as often as possible with our newborn, and Michel's mother was often thrilled to step in for nanny duty so I could pitch in for an afternoon. She was a godsend. While we avidly worked to make the boat a sound vessel with a comfortable living space, we were also hoping to charter the boat on weekends that summer for tourist outings. We hoped it would bring in supplementary income to help defray some of our renovation costs. Since it would have been a bit much for us to lead the outings with a baby on board, Gilbert, our competent sailor friend, agreed to be our charter captain. Many a weekend, while we continued land-based work at home, *Cowabunga* weaved in and out of our local harbor, ferrying summer passersby along the immediate coast. We didn't earn a fortune from it, but it was helpful in keeping our budget afloat.

In between those tourist trips, we continued devoting weekends, holidays, and vacation time to working on the boat and taking short sailing trips for the three of us. By the next springtime, Sean was a year old, and we had more or less worked out the kinks of having a young child on board, "baby proofing" as best we could (i.e., attaching netting around the deck between the stanchions, adding a high sideboard for his bed, using a harness when necessary on deck).

With summer just around the corner, we decided to put our words into action and try living on the boat full time. What better time to start than in the warm weather? So by July of 1980, we moved onto the boat while docked in our homeport of Le Verdon. On weekends, we sailed. During the workweek, Michel tended to architecture projects at his office. The summer living experiment went so well that we decided to take things to the next step and move onto the boat for the remainder of the year. Could we make it through a winter?

We worked out a lot of the daily living details over the summer: the logistics of hauling the groceries and a toddler from the car to the dock to the boat, storing provisions, cooking with only a select few pots and pans in a doll-sized kitchen, rationing water, resizing some sheets to fit the trapezoidal form of our bed.

We acquired a kerosene heater for cold winter nights, took care not to slip on the icy deck in the mornings, and dealt with accumulated condensation from our breathing while sleeping in our very small aft cabin. Providing enough time for Sean to stretch out on land, most often at his grandparents' place, was another priority. Oblivious to his circumstances of a more constrained living space than most children, Sean easily learned how to walk both on the boat and on land.

Despite the constraints of living in such small quarters, Sean took quite naturally to living on *Cowabunga*. His easygoing and curious nature was a good fit for the lifestyle. Like all toddlers, Sean constantly asked questions, of course favoring the eternal "why." He always wanted to know what project Michel was working on and if he could help. Sean was also (and still is) a talker—a very social animal. He never hesitated to tell anyone in earshot that he lived on a boat, and that her name was *Cowabunga*. Since "playdates" didn't exist in those days in France, and there weren't a lot of other toddlers around at the time, Sean experienced a fairly concentrated dose of our boat life. This, along with his bilingual ability to bounce between English and French, were both molding factors for his future.

By the time our third summer on the boat came around, Sean was two years old and we began thinking about baby number two. We had a daily living routine worked out by then, and the renovation and maintenance work had become a way of life. Sean was ready for preschool in the fall. It was time he mixed with other children on a regular basis, and be exposed to people, routines, and events outside of our close family sphere. We hoped this would prepare him for a change in his world. I felt ready to face the challenge of being pregnant on board. Throughout the next winter, my midsection expanded and physically managing Sean while walking through the narrow passageways onboard was becoming laborious. Eventually, at about 8 ½ months, I plainly couldn't fit down the main hatch anymore. We decided to stay at my in-laws' place in nearby Montalivet, about a half hour from our dock in Le Verdon. Two weeks later, in March 1982, Brendan appeared on the scene true to his due date.

After a week at the hospital (as was customary in France at the time), we brought Brendan directly home to *Cowabunga*, the only home he was to know until we arrived in California eight years later. In the eternal debate of what is nurture versus nature, it's hard to know how much of life on *Cowabunga* influenced Brendan later in his life, or how much of who he is now is innate. Brendan is fiercely independent and has always been his own person—not easily influenced or won over. He is very pensive, and I can't help but think that his first eight years deeply reflect his novel start in life and is integral to his spirit today.

Soon after Brendan was born, Michel was approached by an architect who was interested in buying his firm. We decided the moment had come to leave, ready or not (it was more "not" than ready). We would never be completely prepared. There would always be something more to do, something else to finish, always more money that could be put away. But at some point, one has to make a leap of faith.

We used every waking moment of that summer to get ready to go. Since some of the interior renovations proved not as workable as we thought, Michel pulled out his tools once again for some last-minute adjustments and refinements. We had sails and equipment to buy. We had shopping to do and a storage space to wring out of thin air. How much food and water would we need? Would we use all those baby bottles? Where could I store more diapers? Which toys should we keep? We had to sell our cars, give up the apartment, dispose of the washing machine, pare down our wardrobes, buy some proper foul weather gear... Our to-do list continued to expand. During the final week, we had an actual pallet of food and goods delivered to my in-law's house, and drove carload after carload up to the boat, storing each load properly before retrieving the next. I only bought the final fresh fruit and vegetables at the last minute, the day before our departure.

Eventually, the months whittled down to weeks, then days. Our friends and family had witnessed our commitment to the project over the previous three years, and their reactions ran the gamut of emotions. Some never believed we would really go, most were sad, others were proud. Michel's father was perhaps the most bewildered of all by this folly. His son had become an architect—a "someone." Papy, as we called him, was proud of his son, and for the life of him he could not understand why Michel was "throwing it all away." Mamie, Michel's mother, was distraught. She was close to our boys, and we to her. Although she knew our departure was imminent when the pallet of goods was delivered to their door, we avoided telling her the exact date and time we planned to leave. Michel thought it better to tell her we had left once we were out at sea, via the marine radio.

My parents were a bit more accepting of our folly, especially my dad who tended to be attracted to bold endeavors. They never criticized our choice or passed judgement. I am fairly certain, however, that they assumed sailing would be a passing fancy, and that we would soon settle down as most young families do, or should.

Despite all our parents' misgivings, all four were proud of our adventure and willingly recounted our whereabouts and experiences to their friends. Michel's father even kept a map of the world taped to the wall in his den, which he updated with push pins marking our destinations.

On August 29, 1982, we were ready to sail with the high tide at 3 p.m. At 2 p.m., friends gathered on the dock. Michou hovered with his fishing trawler, ready to escort us out of the harbor. Sean knew we were getting ready to sail, but he couldn't understand the magnitude of what we were about to undertake. We shared hugs, kisses, and goodbyes with our small crowd, promising to meet again farther south, or on the other side of the Atlantic. Some of our friends boarded Michou's boat. We dawdled as long as we dared, and then finally fired up the engine, threw off the lines, and angled the bow out of the harbor.

The first entry of our ship's log was begun by Michel that evening: "...calm night, light breeze, not cold—perfect send off." My journal says: "One dream, one sailboat, 3 1/2 years, two children later, we left today."

CHAPTER TWO

ℱIRST ᴅAYS AT ᴤEA

ℱor Michel and me, our departure was bittersweet. It was a more emotionally wrenching experience than we had anticipated, and both of us were uncharacteristically quiet the first few hours. I had imagined that we would be exuberant, high-fiving each other once we left the harbor. Instead, I avoided talking much for fear I would start crying.

I didn't quite understand my feelings initially, but the new constant of the endless horizon helped me sort out my jumble of emotions. Although we had crossed the Bay of Biscay several times in the past and had spent nights at sea on previous coastal trips, this time was different. It was a permanent change. For both of us, it took four days at sea to digest it all, and only then did we begin looking forward to what may lay ahead. We had to find our bearings and a way to recreate a sense of belonging in our new world.

We also needed to adjust to our new daily routine without a morning alarm clock. Well, to be honest, with an infant and toddler on board, we hadn't used an actual alarm clock in a while. But still, we reveled in the fact that we didn't have to rise and shine for someone else's imperatives: appointments, business meetings, or deadlines. We also soon discovered that once we were living and sailing full time, as opposed to our most recent erratic life—splitting daily routines between land-based occupations and weekend sailing outings and boat renovation projects—our new all-boat, all-the-time routine absolutely agreed with us. No, it wasn't always pure bliss. In fact, it was a lot of work, but we were delighted to be doing it.

When at sea, the sextant sun sights constituted the bedrock of our navigation. Several times a day, Michel and I would take secure positions on deck, he with the sextant in hand, and me with a stopwatch. Through the sextant's viewfinder, he would attempt to align the sun with the horizon, which was quite a feat since the boat was always bobbing and weaving. Once Michel decided he had a good fix on the sun and horizon, he called it out to me and ideally, at that very same instant, I clicked the stopwatch, capturing the exact time of his sight. We repeated this several times, and Michel would then calculate each fix according to his precise marine charts and tables, plotting each position on our sea chart. Then he would take the average of those recorded fixes that fell around the same spot, estimating our position. This at-sea job of navigation was juggled around the daily routine of cooking, eating, sleeping, changing diapers, bathing, etc.—just like life and chores on land.

Once we arrived at a destination, we slipped into a shore-life mode of operating, where our comfort and routines were dictated by whether we were anchored or tied up to a dock. Our first priorities were to refill our provisions and water tanks, wash clothes, and get the boys on land for some well-earned running around, boy-energy style! One of *my* first priorities upon arriving in a new port was to scope out the easiest access to water. It became an obsession. Like the captain of times past with his telescope, I would immediately scan the shore closest to where we were anchored or docked for a water out-let—any outlet! If Michel were to go on land first to see about port entry documents and formalities, my first instruction to him was al-ways: "Find the water!"

With luck, there would be a nearby hose or faucet on land that we could use without restrictions. Free-and-easy access to water was a prized commodity. We needed it for cooking, washing, and bathing, and we tried to avoid using our onboard water reserves as much as possible when we knew we wouldn't have easy access to fresh water. Most of the time, we were downright miserly with it. At sea, we would wash the dishes and ourselves with salt water, followed by a quick fresh water rinse. Whether or not water was freely available and accessible on land determined the ease or difficulty of our coming days in port, and consequently our enjoyment of the place.

Above all, our children's needs and their schedules came first, and that wasn't always easy. Brendan had a full and constant infant sched-ule, and the two boys' moods impacted us whether we were at sea or in port. Would they play well together today? Would they hold off on a crisis while we executed a sailing maneuver? Would they have good, long naps? Would they cooperate for an outing on land? Would an easy grocery shopping trip be in the cards?

Sean and Brendan each took to the change of living and sailing on *Cowabunga* full time in their own stride. Sean wasn't going to preschool anymore once we left France, and he was genuinely excited by all the new places we arrived in. Within just the first few weeks of our new life on the move, he also became impassioned with fishing and tweak-ing ropes from the cockpit, imitating our maneuvers with the sails.

Sean was a bit sensitive, at times, to the movement of the boat upon first setting sail for a new passage. If things started out a bit rough, he would snuggle comfortably in his bed for a while, as if in-stinctively letting his body incorporate the new rhythm and settling in

to the change. Once underway, however, Sean returned to always being busy. He tied knots, lowered and raised our naval signal flags,
tweaked the line for his toy tugboat that trailed alongside us in the
water, surveyed his fishing line, observed our anchoring maneuvers,
obsessed over the dolphins, and built churches and lighthouses with his
Lego blocks.

Sean was also beginning to notice sunrises, sunsets, and the rare
moments when the moon and the sun shared the sky at dawn. He began to understand the concept of a coastline and notable promontory
points, and how those figured in our course. He was intrigued by maps
and charts, and how landmarks on paper translated into what he saw
outside. He liked to have us pinpoint where we were on a map of the
world he had in one of his children's books, and then he would sit next
to Brendan indicating our position to him. Sean was becoming used to
the incline of the boat under sail and understood when things just
weren't right with the wind or the sea.

"La mer est méchante," he would say in French. *The sea is being
mean.*

Brendan, at this infant stage, seemed oblivious to any new scenery
or harbor changes since up to that point, the boat had been his only
home. When we were at anchor, the boat always had softer rocking
motion, which captivated Brendan. There was never a need to rock
him to sleep since the constant rocking of the boat was ready-made for
a baby. He also took a new interest in the dancing flames of the kerosene lamps.

Our days were amply filled. Nap times, the wind, the weather,
our night watches, sometimes anchor watch (when the holding ground
was doubtful), equipment repairs, and the very long list of our ongoing
and future ambitious projects to better the boat along with cooking,
eating, and sleeping kept us occupied at all times. We also had to remember to keep an eye on the battery charge which we maintained

with a solar panel and a wind generator, along with running the engine. It was vital since it was our source of electricity on board for the lights, navigational electronics, and radio communication. It was also important to monitor the status of our fresh produce, yogurt, and bread for the days ahead, depending on our accessibility to land. There were no holes to fill with idleness. Our needs and wants were reduced to the very simple basics of life. We stopped the world and got off, and it made such down-to-earth sense!

In this new life and our day-to-day routine, Michel and I couldn't escape each other. We were now together constantly, all day long, every day. Yet, despite being in a very confined space for our family, it worked. There is something to be said, however, for our being "young and in love" at the time. We talked, we planned, we dreamed. We relished being around each other, and not having our time chopped up by the annoying nine-to-five workweek schedule that had plagued us in our former life. At that point, we had been married seven years, and all was quite blissful—even with a toddler and an infant.

At the same time, it was important that Michel and I both had personal alone time, and we managed to carve that out during our night watches and afternoon down time while Brendan napped and Sean busied himself with projects. Private reading time, sewing, meal planning, trying new recipes, fishing, honing navigation skills, carpentry work, and a few cat-naps were all slipped in, all aside from our ever-present parenting duties. Alone time was, and still is today, essential for me. I came to welcome my watches, and savor the early morning hours at sunrise before everyone else woke up.

We did have our occasional arguments, of course. But stomping off for a walk around the block or isolating oneself in a corner wasn't an option. Michel always knew when I was angry—at the flick of a switch, I would spew out a battery of swear words in English. Anger in French isn't fulfilling for me. It sounds too nice. Once our bilingual battle had fizzled out, we would give each other the silent treatment for a few hours. After that, the solitude of a good four-hour night watch softened our tempers and often helped us see the "lesson learned" for whatever the dispute was.

Many such families or couples didn't last against these odds. They weren't able to make the good times overshadow the bad. We came across several abandoned boats and others for sale, littered across various ports-of-call. Dashed dreams and adventures, all stories of their own. We were wary of this happening to us and had applied ourselves to the study of this negative, yet possible outcome of a seafaring life well before we left France. During our two years of experimental onboard living prior to our departure, we had met other families and couples as they passed through our homeport of Le Verdon, or during our brief weekend jaunts up and down the French Atlantic coast. We visited their boats, saw how they did things, talked and exchanged ideas over cocktails and dinners. We read many books about families' experiences, their tips, their do's and don'ts.

We reached La Coruña, Spain after four nights at sea. Our first night in there gave us a few surprises and revealed a crack or two in our practices. We arrived at night and made the decision to anchor out in the bay rather than closer to the dock or marina. However, in our brief sailing experience, we hadn't had many opportunities to anchor, so there was a good amount of angry yelling that went on between the two of us. Michel was at the bow of the boat, and I was in the cockpit, handling the wheel and the engine. There is some delicate maneuvering to do in order to get the boat in the right position so the anchor can be properly set. Michel was giving me his instructions while shouting into the wind ahead of him. I was 40 ft. behind him at the wheel, and I couldn't hear a thing that he was shouting. Finally, Michel set the anchor down, and after a prudent amount of time to verify that it held well, we called it a night and went to bed. When we got up the next morning, we were not in the same spot where we had anchored.

"Do you think we were this far from the shore last night when we anchored?" I asked Michel. "It's hard to tell in daylight from last night's shore lights."

To our surprise, we had dragged quite a bit during the night because the anchor didn't hold. We were lucky that there was a lot of room in the bay for such a mistake. As we lifted the anchor and maneuvered to reset it, it came out of the water fully hooked into an old discarded mattress! No wonder we drifted along during the night. We were never anchored into the sea floor.

"At least it made for a soft landing," Michel mused.

We needed to learn to anchor better, rethink our procedure, and implement a better system of communication between the two of us. Obviously, we hadn't mastered the art of anchoring yet, and it was proving to be a major point of contention between the two of us, as an argument would instantly flare-up.

From then on, Michel employed hand signals that I could easily see and decipher from my position at the back of the boat or the stern. He motioned his hands forward, backward, to the right and left letting me know how to position *Cowabunga*, as I shifted the engine to counter the wind and current. We really needed to survey the set anchor for at least a half hour before deciding whether we had good holding or not. We eventually became quite adept at this and rarely had any arguments about anchoring after that.

La Coruña proved to be a good starting point. Many sailboats came and went, and many were like us, leaving for the first time after years of preparation. We met people who had even built their own boats, and some were returning home after years of sailing around the world. We found out that we were part of the "Class of '82"—that year's contribution to the annual migration of new adventurers heading south for the first time. There was a whole subculture of enthusiasts of the sea, and now we were part of the wave. We came across many of these boats and families of the "Class of '82" later in our travels, in different countries and different oceans.

Our identity was also transformed here. Our last name, Couvreux, faded away. People would, from then on, know and recognize us as the "famille *Cowabunga*," the "*Cowabunga* family." Everyone became one with the name of their boats and consequently identified as such. We developed close friendships with some families over the years, and never even knew their real last names.

Our next port-of-call after La Coruña, was the Ria de Corcubion, in the Galicia area of Spain, where there are numerous *rias*, or inlets. We tied up to a dock in the protected enclave of Corcubion, just around the edge of Spain that juts out into the Atlantic known as Finisterre, or "land's end." The days were warm and sunny, and I could place Brendan on the deck in his little bouncy chair. I noticed a new shift in his awareness and saw that Brendan was now beginning to enjoy the outside surroundings and the hustle and bustle of the harbor. Since we were centrally located in the port, we were somewhat of an attraction with a baby and small boy on board, especially during the traditional evening Spanish *paseo* hour when families leisurely walk around and relax after their day of work. Sean would implore passersby to help him pull his multi-knotted ropes wrapped around a winch, connected to a line of naval signal flags that he liked to hoist up, as he imitated our maneuvers with the sails.

Up to this point, Sean had been enveloped in a total bilingual cocoon of French and English in our family life. I only spoke English to the boys, and Michel, along with everyone else in their lives thus far, only spoke French. Being introduced to the Spanish language was a new wrinkle for him. We tried to explain to Sean that in this new country, people spoke something different from Mama and Papa and that to say "hello" in Spanish was *hola*. For the few days we were in Corcubion, there was a little boy of about 10 years old who came by daily to enjoy Sean's company. It was our first experience observing how Sean could make friends with children in another country. We welcomed the little boy with "hola." By the next evening, Sean was anxious to see his friend again.

"When is Hola coming?" he asked.

CHAPTER THREE

FAREWELL EUROPE

Anxious to push onward with our journey of discovery, we bid goodbye to Hola and Corcubion, and ambled down the Spanish coast to Portugal by way of a few easy day trips and one-night anchorages. We lingered a bit in Portugal—it was a pleasure to discover. In Portugal, we discovered Porto, the resort town of Figueira da Foz, and finally Lisbon.

The anchorage for Porto was located in the nearby industrial harbor of Leixoes, and it was here that we skirted an early disaster. Leixoes was a small harbor, and there were several boats anchored there. I suddenly awoke because the boat was not bobbing with the same usual rhythm that I was becoming accustomed to while at anchor. I'm a light sleeper, and such dissonant things always seemed to wake me. A sudden squall with powerful winds had whipped up during the night around 4 a.m. I raised myself on my elbows, peeped through the porthole in our aft sleeping cabin and saw that *Cowabunga* was racing past other boats and towards the rocky jetty. I was in a terrified panic! I shook Michel awake, and in a flash, we were on deck in the pelting rain, engine roaring, steering *Cowabunga* clear of the rocks just moments away from certain doom.

We weren't the only ones to avoid disaster that night. Several of us, all having been dragged, were weaving around the harbor at 4 a.m. seeking safer, better-protected spots to re-anchor. Once we got *Cowabunga* resettled, soaked and with our hearts pounding, we reassessed what happened. Coming on the heels of our anchoring mishap in La Coruña, we again doubted our ability to anchor properly. However, upon closer inspection of this storm, Michel realized that the squalls were coming in from the south, and the harbor wasn't well protected from the weather in that direction. We were fairly comforted that it wasn't entirely due to our lack of anchoring technique, but we nevertheless failed to factor in possible issues when anchoring in that particular harbor. We were further distressed when we realized how close we had come to losing *Cowabunga* on the rocks. We had only just begun our dream voyage and couldn't believe that all was almost lost right there in Portugal, so close to our starting point in France.

After Porto, we made an unscheduled stop in Figueira da Foz due to engine problems, the first major breakdown of many more to come. Contrary to the disappointing and fairly disheveled industrial harbor of Leixoes-Porto, Figueira da Foz was a pleasant surprise—a quaint and clean summer tourist town.

Portugal of the 1980s was emerging from a long period of dictatorial regimes and was somewhat in the third world pocket of Europe. It still lacked in modern comforts; horse-drawn carts were common in the streets, as were women carrying basket-laden loads on their heads and babies on their hips. We rarely saw any strollers, and we garnered many a curious look as Michel carried Brendan in our backpack-style baby carrier. Cod is the national dish of Portugal, so we also discovered a new odor as street vendors hawked dried and salted cod everywhere.

Once in the harbor of Figueira da Foz, Michel went on an exploratory expedition to find someone who could help us out with our
engine. At the small tourist information office in town, he discovered
there was a local chapter of the Lions Club, of which Michel was a
member back home. Luckily, one of the chapter's members, Mario
Cardoza, was a garage mechanic, and he immediately came to our aid.
He and his family were most generous and congenial hosts. Aside from
competently repairing our engine, Mario took us to his home and insisted that we use the washing machine. They even treated us out to
dinner and a tour of the sleepy village in the hopeful midst of transforming to a seaside resort town. Street corner cod filets vendors
brushed up against newcomers targeting leisure beach weekends. All
this unexpected kindness was just the medicine we needed, and we
were grateful for it during the week that we were there to repair our
engine.

Our next stop was Lisbon, just a day's sail down the coast from
Figueira da Foz, about 125 miles away. Lisbon was a major gathering
spot for cruisers as they regrouped before heading out to various pre-
Caribbean destinations like Madeira, the Canary Islands, or the
Azores. This wouldn't be the case for us, though, as we planned to
continue down the coast to Gibraltar, our final European destination.
In Lisbon, we were corralled into the "foreign yacht" harbor, centrally
located near the heart of town with about 50 other cruisers of all na-
tionalities.

From our deck in the Lisbon harbor, Sean immediately spied a
"train"—actually the metro—and he was anxious to give it a whirl.
We sensed that our children were sometimes more irate than they
should be, which I think was due to lack of personal, individual attention. It was easy to get too wrapped up in everyday chores, repairs,
and the "to-do" list, and the kids could feel that. We needed to take
more days off here and there, and devote more time exclusively to

them. They needed time in parks, walks on land, and local adventures like discovering a zoo. So for our week in Lisbon, we paid particular attention to this. Sean was thrilled and all smiles with his first train ride.

We already saw changes in Sean and Brendan in just these two months. Sean began to notice coastal landmarks and understand that changes in the wind necessitated maneuvers to modify the sails. He was learning what purpose the ropes (sheets or halyards) served. Brendan, now almost seven months, was still in his own discovery mode of the world. I do wonder, though, if he ever found it strange that the scenery outside was never the same.

From Lisbon, we sailed back into Spain down to Cadiz. We targeted Cadiz mainly as a rest stop to break up the trip from Lisbon to Gibraltar, our next stop, and to prepare ourselves mentally for the infamous currents of the Strait of Gibraltar. The reputation was that the currents changed suddenly and could be erratic. To this day, Cadiz remains most memorable in our minds for another barely averted catastrophe.

We were sailing out of the harbor at sunset for our overnight sail to Gibraltar. For a short trip like this, it was easier to sail at night since we wouldn't be burdened by Brendan's daily routine (bottles, diaper changes).

The boys were playing calmly below, and I was planning to get dinner on once we were underway. As we cleared the harbor and the ocean opened before us, we set the sails and cut the engine. It was choppy with some swell—fairly typical. I took the wheel so Michel could set the wind vane pilot that would steer the boat by itself at the stern of the boat. We had a routine for this, and I assumed he was doing his usual tasks in getting the ropes ready. As I held the course, looking straight ahead, I was awaiting Michel's customary instructions for steering and holding the course. I kept waiting…but he didn't say anything, which was odd. I finally turned around to see what was going on, and there he was, sprawled out on the back of the boat with a bloodied head.

"Michel!" I yelled.

No answer.

He was unconscious. I had to go to him, but I couldn't just let go of the wheel. If I did, we'd veer off course, the sails would flap around or get caught the wrong way, and even more trouble or damage could ensue. I could see the boom of the mizzen mast flailing about. Due to an oversight, neither one of us had properly tied the mizzen boom down as we usually did, and the choppy swell had sent it on a collision course with Michel's head!

I finally chose to leave the wheel and rushed to shake Michel and assess his wound, all the while glancing up to keep tabs on our position. He quickly came to and was woozy for a short while, and had a big, bloody bump. Thankfully, there was no need for stitches. I ran back and forth between him and the wheel several times, keeping us right with the wind, while helping him to the cockpit, blotting his bloody head.

"Are you OK?" I repeatedly asked in a panic. "How many fingers do you see?" I waved my index finger in front of his eyes.

"Oui, ça va, je pense," Michel said. *Yes, I'll be OK, I think.*

We realized how lucky we were that he wasn't knocked overboard and that I might have realized it too late if that had been the case. Later that night, though, when I was off watch and Michel was on, I still wasn't at ease. I worried about a concussion or some other latent damage. But by the next morning, he was back into the swing of things, other than the nasty bump on his head. Now we would remember: check and double check that any possible flying object is always secured in its rightful place. This wasn't news to us, but now we really understood the importance of it.

Onward to Gibraltar, our last stop in Europe and our gateway to Africa!

A little after the noon hour on the day of our arrival, we saw Morocco and the African coast for the first time. It was quite a feeling to be sailing between two continents: Africa to our starboard, Europe to our port. On the marine radio, we were excited to hear ship traffic from Casablanca, Radio Tangier, Tarifa, and Gibraltar. It was clear and sunny with calm blue waters. Perfect. Then suddenly we heard the distinct sounds of choppy water. It sounded as if someone turned on a faucet full force. Looking behind us, we watched the surface ripple suddenly, galloping toward us. It caught up with us, undulated under us, and surrounded us like a pot of boiling water.

So this was the quirky current we had heard of and read about. It wasn't uncomfortable, nor dangerous—just very odd. It was as if a line had been drawn in the sea, dividing calm water from an agitated frontier, creating an inoffensive, almost cute "tidal" wave.

We reveled in the fun of Gibraltar, discovering the Rock for about ten days. It was an unlikely mix of European cultures. Awash in a colorful blend, there were traditional British "bobbies" who directed traffic, veiled Moroccan woman, elegant in their glittery traditional robes, and an eclectic international yachtie crowd docked at the foot of the Rock. I was incredulous of the venerable monument rising right out of the water. It was the real deal, not the Prudential Financial logo I had seen on TV in my childhood days.

We biked to the actual Rock and encountered some of the famous resident monkeys (Barbary macaques), walked the town streets, and witnessed the Changing of the Guard ceremony at the government headquarters.

On one outing Michel earned a well-deserved scolding from one corner constable. He rode past the officer on a bicycle, against traffic on a busy one-way street, with Sean seated in the front child's seat braced behind the handlebars, and Brendan in the baby pack hoisted on Michel's shoulders like a circus-type, human pyramid.

"Tweeeet!" the officer hailed Michel with his whistle. "Do you realize how dangerous your stunt is? And with two young children and limited visibility in such busy automobile traffic, you should know better for everyone's safety," he admonished my wayward husband.

Michel sheepishly admitted to his lapse of good judgement and continued on foot, pushing Sean along on the bicycle and carrying Brendan on his back.

As was becoming our custom, we alternated tourist activities and playdates for Sean and Brendan with grocery shopping and boat maintenance duties. This time I had some housekeeping details to tend to. Brendan was quickly outgrowing his infant sleeping arrangement, and I needed to sew a new lee cloth for his bed. A lee cloth is a canvas that hooks from under the mattress and attaches to the ceiling so he couldn't fall out, especially with the boat in motion. I used a larger version of this canvas for the main cabin couches to give Brendan a safe interior "playpen" area while we were under sail. I also had to make some mosquito nets for our beds, along with Moroccan and Senegalese flags to fly upon our arrival in those countries, as prescribed by international maritime law. Some port authorities could be very put out by a boat's lack of courtesy in neglecting to fly the host country's flag, and they would go so far as to create some genuine red-tape headaches for the offending yacht.

Getting into Gibraltar was easy and straightforward; getting out was another story. Due to the unpredictable currents, it was important to time an entry or departure from Gibraltar according to the tide.

For our departure, we thought we had timed it right for the outgoing tide, but we learned otherwise. We kept spinning our wheels, trapped, unable to make any headway out. Finally, after a good eight hours of basically treading water, the Rock was still grandly displayed before us, just as it was when we had set out that morning. We gave up and sailed across the water to the African continent, to the independent and isolated enclave port of Ceuta, which borders Morocco. Although we could still see Gibraltar across the Strait in the distance from the harbor of Ceuta, the day didn't seem as futile if we entered a different harbor for the night.

The next day, we carefully re-read the nautical instructions that gave explicit descriptions—almost to the exact times and distances from the coast—of how the current could change with an outgoing tide, and that one should sidle up to a parallel course depending upon the tidal shifts. We had previously studied this and didn't exactly "pooh-pooh" the information, but we didn't realize how precise it was or that it would have behooved us to follow the instructions to the letter (and to the minute). We performed our second attempt flawlessly. Michel deftly navigated our course, orchestrating our maneuvers and syncing our path with the predicted shifts in the current. The Strait spat us out, and we finally said goodbye to Europe. We turned to face Africa and my, what a feeling that was! We were invigorated, yet slightly uneasy as we headed into the unknown: new territory, new languages, new cultures.

Although we had read a lot of yachties' accounts of sailing to Morocco and heard the wonderful tales of others who spent considerable time there, Michel harbored some hesitations—perhaps even some prejudices—given France's long and tumultuous colonial history in North Africa. Michel's own family history had been affected by the Algerian war for independence since his father had been a combatant in the war. He had been a career officer in the Gendarmerie, the militarized branch of the French police. Michel wasn't sure what to expect in Morocco, or how he would be treated as a Frenchman.

PART TWO

Africa

CHAPTER FOUR

CASABLANCA AND
MOROCCAN CHARM

anding in Africa was another first for us—a new continent.
Not knowing what to expect, many of my night watch hours
were spent imagining what might await us, all framed within the
indelible images from the film "Casablanca,"—the stuff of legends.
Never in my wildest dreams did I ever imagine setting foot there.
Humphrey Bogart and Ingrid Bergman, and a place where "a kiss was
just a kiss" danced in my brain.[1]

My nostalgic reverie was arrested by the reality of sailing into a
filthy and polluted harbor. Tar and fuel-covered wharfs were part of a
mosaic of decrepit buildings, a few half-sunken vessels, a hodge-podge
of ragged stray cats and dogs, and a small posse of fishermen whiling
away the time. It was eerie and somewhat void of life, yet distinct with
telltale signs of a Casablanca from the past.

---

[1] *Casablanca*, 1942 American romantic drama, directed by Michael
Curtiz, staring Humphrey Bogart, Ingrid Bergman, and Paul Henreid

Having arrived in the early afternoon, much of the rest of the day was spent hunting down the proper offices and authorities to fulfill our entry formalities. On the move now for three months, we were getting the hang of how to fulfill these requirements when entering a new country. Every country had its own particular procedures of what paperwork needed to be completed and how. In general, there were customs, immigration, and sometimes health and agriculture regulations to attend to. Sometimes we had to procure a visa prior to arriving, and sometimes they would issue it on the spot.

The procedure in Casablanca turned out to be tedious, and was made even more unpleasant by a customs officer's insistence that we offer him a bottle of whiskey when he came on board and spied our stash purchased in Gibraltar. The word out on the cruising circuit was that whiskey was a very useful currency in Brazil for an exchange of services, so we had bought twelve bottles for later on in our trip. This Moroccan officer was blatant with his request, and Michel respectfully refused to surrender a bottle. There is a fine line between bartering for services and caving in to bribes, and Michel finessed his way through with a straight moral compass.

At this point we played the "American" card. Michel pointed out that since our boat was of American registry, as signified by the American flag in our rigging, the official should bear in mind that we would not hesitate to enlist the assistance of the American consulate on our behalf. Although the officer threatened us with "trouble and complications" if we didn't give him what he wanted, he eventually backed down. Later when Michel was in the harbor customs office for more paperwork, the same official asked once again for some whiskey, this time right in front of his superior. Again, Michel refused and the subject was laid to rest. Michel's systematic refusal to pay bribes most likely cost us in the form of a few extra hours of useless waiting and aggravation as officials invented on-the-spot bureaucratic complications. But within the cruising world, we were aware of the "trickle-down" effect that our actions and behavior could produce for others. Giving in to the culture of bribery wouldn't do any favors for sailors who came after us.

Anxious to get on land, we spent our first evening in the Medina quarter, a lively contrast to the forsaken harbor. We weren't disappointed. The Medina bustled and bartered, with gritty streets and glittery mazes while whining traditional strains of Arab music called people to prayer. Handicapped and mutilated men, women, and children languished throughout the streets with outstretched hands. Vendors hawked wares in labyrinths of stalls and souks, grouped by trades: tailors, weavers, fruit and vegetable sellers. A curious parade of veiled women passed while balancing trays of flatbread dough on their heads, and then scurried into sunken peephole entrances. Thoroughly intrigued, we stooped to look in and beheld underground, centuries-old, wood-fired ovens—community ovens for baking household bread.

Obviously Westerners, we stood out like coarse threads within this finely woven tapestry. We elicited many a stare, especially with Brendan bouncing in his backpack. Sean was a magnet (dare I say chick magnet?) as women were drawn to his deep auburn hair, reaching out to touch it. One woman approached us and cradled Brendan's bare feet in her hands, worried that he would catch cold. For us, this October evening was warm.

As we meandered in the lively confusion, the stares melted into smiles, hellos, oft-spoken French, and invitations to taste tangerines and breads, or just talk. Brendan couldn't get enough of all the sights. He sat ramrod straight in his pack, wide-eyed, taking it all in. Sean was a trooper, carrying on as we walked a lot. Being only three, however, he suddenly had the urge to pee. There, standing before a vendor's stall and a bakery, we were at a loss! Before we had time to figure something out, a gentleman behind the stall heard Michel and I debating the issue, and he suddenly volunteered a solution, whisking Sean away to a building just across the way. By the time we realized what had happened and began to panic, the man returned with a smiling Sean in his arms. Intrigued, we peppered Sean with our questions as to what their private living quarters were like. Relieving himself, it seems, was no big deal. He just aimed for "a hole in the ground."

Our stay in Casablanca was unfortunately brief, having boxed ourselves into a tight timeline to be in Dakar by Christmas. Although it was only the end of October at this point, we still had much sea to cover with intended stops in Agadir, Morocco, and the Canary Islands before arriving in Senegal.

After a few wonderful days of true "kid time" in Casablanca, involving parks, Moroccan sweets, and a café or two, we left without incident. The authorities duly and politely stamped our exit papers (knowing once and for all they wouldn't get our whiskey), and no ocean counter currents hindered our departure. The sail down the coast was a welcomed downwind leg, with striking scenery. This was the extreme western edge of the Sahara Desert, and it was incredible to see the sand dunes spilling into the edge of the sea. I kept expecting Lawrence of Arabia to come galloping down a crease in the dunes, on his majestic mount and enveloped by his flowing robes. The sails began to take on an orange hue as red sandy dust accumulated in the folds of our sails and canvas covers. The sun was sometimes even veiled by an orange-red pall cast by the dust-laden desert horizon.

Nestled at the foot of Morocco's Atlas Mountains, about 315 miles south of Casablanca, lies Agadir. Rebuilt after the original city was mostly flattened by a catastrophic earthquake in 1960, it is now a winter tourist destination. But in 1982, there were only a few hints of what it would become in the future. There was no pleasure craft marina then, so we sailed into a dirty harbor that reeked of rotten fish, thanks to a sardine processing facility situated right on the wharf. This rendered the water into a mass of smelly goo as the waste was just dumped into the harbor. *Cowabunga* was rather pitiful, instantly encased in this gunk, and the hull became outlined with a yellow greasy film. The smell was something akin to that of oil lingering in the kitchen from a deep-fried meal the night before—only much more pungent. I had to cover my nose so I could fall asleep at night.

Belying this initial repelling impression, however, was the extreme generosity, courtesy, and genuine friendliness of the locals. They wanted to tell us about their city, their culture, their religion, their customs, their language. The post office attendant bid Michel to share tea with him (not an easy feat for Michel since he really dislikes tea!) while he waited for a phone line to become available. Someone in the harbor lent Michel a scooter to pick up a load of tangerines. A shoe cobbler in the open-air market repaired Michel's broken flip-flop for a pittance. All this took Michel off guard and melted away his hesitations and admitted prejudices. We were won over by these gentle, sincere people. Morocco seduced us.

With our load of tangerines (and definitely no sardines), we headed out for the Canary Islands, as well as—unintentionally—our first major storm since leaving France. With an average wind speed of 50 knots, or about 60 mph, this tempest was nothing to sneeze at. The sea was huge, but rather than high cresting, foamy waves that would have normally been the case in such a storm, the sea was an expansive, oddly impressive swell, with a volume and height the likes of which I had never seen. Surprising myself, I wasn't as scared as I'd thought I might be. Most likely because the sea wasn't in a frenzy—although I was definitely nervous! I was annoyed with Michel because he just went to our bunk to sleep it off, figuring there was nothing we could do other than wait it out. He was right, but still, how could he just sleep through all that?

Sean was a bit seasick at first, but not afraid. Brendan was more annoyed that he kept getting knocked down in his play area. I found it interesting that neither Sean nor Brendan ever got seasick prior to learning how to walk. Once they were walking, though, they both had rare, occasional bouts of seasickness. I attribute this to the fact that their sense of equilibrium must not have been well established, and thus seasickness didn't affect them until their bodies had a real sense of gravity and balance.

The next morning, after the storm abated, I couldn't get over the lingering height and volume of the swells. I popped my head outside the companionway to gauge the situation and saw a cargo ship nearby. A mountainous swell towered above us, the cargo teetering on the top of the rolling wave. Then it slid down into the trough of a vast valley below before we, in turn, rolled and shifted up to the top. It seemed like a slow-motion roller coaster or the movement of swimming pool water during an earthquake. It was made of exaggerated proportions, something one might see in a cartoon. Having been blown off course for 24 hours, we were able to verify our position through VHF radio contact with the cargo and got back on track to the Canary Islands.

We knew we couldn't do the Canary Islands justice with our time constraints, so we concentrated on just one of the Spanish archipelago's seven islands: Lanzarote, a true surprise. Austere and captivating with its black volcanic desert beauty, there were miles of black sand, hardened lava fields, and spectacular vistas. There were even camel caravans for tourist promenades and curious vineyards that peppered the landscape.

After a quick restocking of provisions on the nearby island of Gran Canaria, we trekked onward for the week-long sail to Dakar, Africa's westernmost point on the Atlantic coast.

It was still early in our adventure, and Michel and I were still learning things about the boat, navigating as a team, determining a good system for our watches, dealing with stress, and adjusting anchoring tactics. My stint on night watch was always a good period of "down time," to read and gather my thoughts after a busy daily schedule. Cliché as it may seem, the starry night sky was awe-inspiring. Far from city lights, total blackness enveloped everything, and I often contemplated this phenomenon. It was truly like looking at a planetarium dome, only this was the real deal.

The hardest part of being on watch was staying awake. Then of course once off watch and in bed, I was so eager to grab those precious hours of rest that it was hard to fall asleep. One evening, I had finally fallen asleep after Michel took over watch duty. Being in this pre-digital music era of the 1980s, he was listening to our Walkman with his headphones. Suddenly I awoke to agonizing groans and short intermittent yelps. Worried, I quickly popped my head out of the hatch.

"Michel, what's wrong?" I said.

"I'm just singing. Why?"

"You scared me half to death. I thought you were in pain!"

His singing with the Walkman was not like singing in the shower.

The boys were growing and changing, and so our daily routine evolved. When we first set sail from France, Sean was edging out of nap time, but it was still a part of Brendan's routine, and that structured the whole family's day. Brendan was also quickly rolling through his baby stages: new teeth, learning to crawl, exploring in and around the boat—prompting us to stay one step ahead of him in installing safety measures. He was also beginning to assert himself with determination, long memory, impatience, whereas Sean was becoming a social chatterbox and a promising fisherman. He had just recently caught his first fish and was duly proud.

Our deadline to make it to Dakar had been reliant on obligations to meet friends there from France, and we found a valuable lesson in this: Don't make plans for specific dates too far in advance. It was the end of November, and our timeline to be in Dakar had restricted us too much. Too many unknowns can and do come into play when sailing, and we needed to learn to give a wider berth to those eventualities. No sooner had we left Gran Canaria, still motoring out of the harbor channel and setting our sails, when the engine quit. Permanently. We had no time to go back and deal with the problem, so we just set the course for Dakar and decided to deal with it when we arrived.

CHAPTER FIVE

U.S. Navy to the Rescue

We made it to Dakar, Senegal. We were a long way from France, a long way from Europe, a long way from the States—a long way from home any way we looked at it. Following our unexpectedly warm welcome in Morocco, we were now eager to get to this sub-Saharan part of Africa with a renewed sense of cautious optimism. Although a separate and independent country, Senegal still depended greatly on French infrastructure and largesse, lending the impression that it maintained close ties to France and thus a feeling of being a frontier outpost. Yet, there were palpable tensions.

Dakar was our last stop in Africa and the springboard for our departure across the Atlantic to Rio de Janeiro, Brazil. But our arrival in Dakar was not what we hoped for by arriving with a dead engine. Michel was able to diagnose the problem as a broken piston valve, based on his experience with this problem earlier in Portugal. The problem was entering an unfamiliar harbor with narrow channels, maneuvering only with our sails.

Dakar was dirty, dusty, industrial, and hostile. Upon our approach, we called up the harbormaster on the VHF "ship-to-shore" radio, explaining our maneuverability problem and inquiring as to the layout of the harbor for a sailing approach. Communication was scratchy. The radio connection wasn't good, and we weren't able to explain that Michel believed the problem to be a broken piston valve. They did offer to come out and tow us in, but that wasn't a good idea given the kind of boat they had, and there might have been a hefty fee to pay. So we agreed to sail into the harbor entrance as far as we could while maintaining ample maneuverability, and then they could pilot us from that point.

We came into the harbor and were met by a *pilotine*. We didn't know where to dock, so we just let them spirit us away towards a bleak wharf. As we readied the dock lines to tie up to shore, we rounded a corner and smack in front of us was a huge U.S. Navy ship—the U.S.S. *O'Bannon*—with a big American flag unfurled and flying in all its glory. What would the U.S. Navy be doing here? In a flash, Michel was inspired and instructed the pilot crew to deposit us directly behind the U.S.S. *O'Bannon*.

We tied *Cowabunga* up sturdily, and once we took stock of our situation, Michel announced to me that now the ball was in my court. "It's your country, go see what they can do."

We needed a competent, honest mechanic, and it was dawning on us at this point that we wouldn't easily find that in this port. Not having a clue how one approaches such a ship or its personnel, I walked up the gangplank and explained our engine situation to a sailor who greeted me. I asked if there might be someone who could take a look at our engine and help figure out a solution. All I had to do was ask. It was magic! Within a half hour, our boat was teeming with U.S. sailors of every persuasion.

Not only were there mechanics, but innumerable others who tended to our every need for a week. They filled up our food lockers, refreshed our water tanks, insisted we steal an evening out while they babysat Sean and Brendan, and they even designated a night watchman just for our sailboat. Not only did they give the engine a thorough repair and tune-up, they also re-wired the motor's electrical circuit. The ship's commander made a special stop to ensure we had all that we needed, and the U.S. Ambassador in Dakar, en route to the U.S.S. *O'Bannon*, stopped his limousine to pay us a courtesy visit.

It seems that the U.S.S *O'Bannon* was on a goodwill tour in Africa. In Dakar, they had just finished helping with some painting and repair projects at local schools and other organizations. They were as surprised to see another American vessel in this harbor as we were to see them, and it forged a unique experience and friendships for all of us.

We became particularly close with three sailors, "Pops," Randy, and Jack, who directed the work. Randy took a keen liking to our boys and developed a great rapport with them. Brendan was still very much a baby at nine-months, but Randy had a way with him. Sean was thrilled to have someone else to prattle on to since he was never one to hold back on a conversation.

Apart from our friendly encounter with the U.S.S. *O'Bannon*, our first taste of Dakar via the industrial harbor was not pleasant. We were harangued and solicited all day by locals who loitered on the wharf, every day and into the night. They were insistent. It was hard to sit outside on the deck as passersby relentlessly hawked their wares or sought handouts. It was hard to stay down below since it was so unbearably hot and humid. It was hard to eat while they so obviously wanted food and whatever else caught their eye. Some of them even brazenly jumped onto our deck and tried to steal items right in front of us. We were constantly on edge. The crew of the U.S.S. *O'Bannon* quickly mounted the guard with a 24-hour watchman, and a bright, glaring spotlight, allowing us some peace of mind at night.

Once the repairs were finished, we were anxious to get out of the hot, dusty, industrial harbor and scoot around the corner to the Lagoon, a protected anchorage where other cruising yachts were anchored. This was a calmer, friendlier place, and more conducive to preparing for our Atlantic passage. We were able to spend time with friends and acquaintances we had made along the way before our next sailing leg. As we prepared to leave the wharf, Randy, Pops, and Jack were given permission by their superior officer to accept our invitation and accompany us on board for the short trip around the jetty to the Lagoon. We were pleased to have them. We also hailed the U.S.S. *O'Bannon* and were allowed to go on board to pay our respects and deepest gratitude to Commander Kibble. He treated us like dignitaries, receiving us in the ship's wardroom, serving us coffee and presenting us with two souvenir U.S.S. *O'Bannon* caps as gifts. We, in turn, presented him a bottle of fine Bordeaux wine from our secret stash. We could never thank him and his crew enough. They saved us an immense amount of worry, time, and money, and made me feel proud of my country.

The next day, our three sailors stood in their military stance at the bow of *Cowabunga*. Navy rules stipulate that any time a U.S. Navy sailor is away from his ship, he must "dress in his full dress whites." We made quite an impression sailing into the Lagoon anchorage with our own personal, uniformed escorts, standing in a salute stance on the deck of *Cowabunga*.

CHAPTER SIX

CHRISTMAS IN DAKAR

Close and convenient to Dakar proper, we basked in the relief of the Lagoon, where the heat was reduced thanks to a calm, constant breeze that fanned us. The blue water was soothing, and it was also nice to reintroduce ourselves to the camaraderie of the cruising community. The sharing of advice and food, loaning of tools, and the secure feeling of belonging enveloped us. Comfort came with the warm evening flicker of the surrounding bobbing cabin lights.

Food—the consumption, preparation, and anticipation of—was an overriding preoccupation and pastime. Not only for us, but in the sailing community in general. Not only did we need to find food (not always easy), but we were often confronted with new and exotic foods, and challenged as to how to prepare them given the confines of a galley kitchen. When out to sea, thinking about and planning meals gave us something to look forward to, and it was always a topic of conversation when we got together with others in port. We traded tips for how to create something gourmet in spite of our limited methods.

A pressure cooker turned out to be a most valuable and widely used item amongst cruisers. It lent itself to a myriad of uses from serving as a canning device to creating stews, yogurts, and even pitching in as an oven of sorts to make bread. It doubled as a safety device, cooking whole meals encapsulated and enclosed within its secure space as we sailed along.

Aside from meals already being the highlight of our sailing life, the importance of food in our "boathold" (as opposed to "household") was amplified by the French food factor. Eating and the meal itself have never been just necessities, they are part of a lifetime of customs and cultural norms.

I wasn't always a cook, nor terribly interested in food as a pastime as the French are. I only became an enlightened convert once I lived in France and learned innumerable cooking skills and tips from my French mother-in-law, Mamie, to whom I am eternally grateful. She demystified much of the French cooking mystique, as I would simply observe what she did and ask her questions. Much of French cooking is just getting back to basics with simple ingredients and simple techniques. It translated well to a subsistent and sustainable life on a boat.

However, food is a passion with the French, and living on a boat was not an excuse to skimp. No freeze-dried packets, ramen noodles, Spam, or instant mashed potatoes for us. No sir! I cooked quiches, pizzas, clams and mussels, fish, calamari, roasted chickens, stews, tarts, flans, and chocolate cakes. I relished baking and gave my onboard oven a good workout. The open-air village markets we happened upon were colorful and lively, and offered new and different foods to experiment with. There were star fruits, passion fruits, and huge glossy avocados in Brazil. Tall burlap bags of fluorescently pigmented spices carpeted the markets in Morocco, and later we came upon live iguanas for cooking for sale in the market stalls of Cayenne, French Guiana.

And always, no matter where we went, there was an abundance of fresh fish.

Contact with local Senegalese citizens was often unfortunately tense. As in many former colonies, Senegal, too, bears the scars of the former white-dominated social order and government. The Senegalese population and the white French expats distrusted each other, although their relationships intertwined daily through jobs, schools, and at the marketplace. Young white mothers still enjoyed a class luxury of often having a black housekeeper and a children's nanny or "nounou," who usually received paltry wages. It was as if much of the white population still held to the attitude of being the colonial power of the past.

Consequently, there was always a detectable undercurrent of hostility. A white person was seen as a stuffed wallet, a source of cash. Buy this, buy that, give me this, give me that... In our experiences with street peddlers in other countries up to that point, a simple "no" had sufficed. In the streets of Dakar, "no" left us wide open to an avalanche of rude retorts and enraged confrontations, all thrown at us while we attempted to mind our own business.

Aside from these unpleasant encounters, we had other interesting experiences during an excursion or shopping trip into the city. We met itinerant French and American students, hitchhiking foreigners just passing through, visiting American professors, a Basque fisherman, assorted Non-Governmental Organization (NGO) volunteers, and a few members of CARE and the Peace Corps. This eclectic mix of people speaking English, French, or the local dialect of Oulof added to the color and exotic ambiance of the surroundings.

Given the hostility displayed in Dakar proper, the nearby island of N'Gor had evolved into a refuge for many white tourists, and some of the white Dakar residents who spent their weekends at their getaway bungalows on N'Gor. We learned about this tropical anchorage that hosted a big chain hotel framed by requisite palm-thatched palapa um-brellas, drinks served on the beach, and its very own intimate aqua-blue lagoon. It wasn't our preference for a vacation locale, but a good compromise given our need for a spell of peace. The easy beach access was nice for the kids and proved to be a calm place to return to after running errands in the hot and dusty city. It was comfortable for Sean and Brendan here in N'Gor, less exposed to the open ocean swell at the Lagoon.

At N'Gor we also met Sec, an intriguing and imposing Senegalese native, who owned a snack concession on the beach. Educated, artic-ulate, and well-traveled, he was a fount of information. We enjoyed many long conversations about the relations between African coun-tries and their former colonists, and worldwide politics in general. Having sailed quite a bit himself, he was extremely helpful to us cruis-ers in supplying us with water, directing us to laundry facilities, and providing invaluable tips on local lore.

It was the Christmas holiday season and our first in a tropical loca-tion. For this first holiday away from our families and in an unfamiliar setting, we had arranged to meet Michel's former business partner, Christian, for Christmas in Dakar. Since Christian's brother was sta-tioned in Dakar with the French military, it seemed like a good opportunity for a get-together and a final farewell to Christian before our definitive break from that part of the world.

Although things had been hectic trying to prepare for our Atlantic crossing, it was important to make time for Christmas with the kids. I fell in love with the French version of Christmas when I first experi-enced it with Michel and his family. The ritual of the meal is a daily given in French life, but it takes on far grander proportions for *the* meal of the year, the Christmas Eve feast. This is the time of the year when the French splurge on specialty items or delicacies that are rare or expensive to indulge in regularly. Since there can be many delicious choices, it is a multi-course extravaganza that lasts most of the evening. The children open gifts early in the evening, and then the long leisurely repast begins with raised glasses of champagne.

Christian's brother and his family hosted this traditional French Christmas Eve feast at their home on the French military base. Santa swapped out his sleigh and reindeer for a military helicopter landing on a soccer field at the base. Sean was ecstatic. Other activities for the day included a screening of Disney's *Cinderella* (a real treat for Sean since we had no television on board).

Michel surprised me with a pair of custom-made hoop earrings. He recounted how he had spotted a curious group of tall, black-robed Moors from neighboring Mauritania in the marketplace one day. Huddled around a fierce fire, they were creating silver jewelry. Michel, with his keen architectural sense of artistry, spied some sleek handmade silver bracelets and thought they would be equally nice as earrings. These artisans were able to transform the bracelets into earrings right then and there over their fire. I still wear those lovely pieces today.

After our Christmas celebration, we got back to the task of preparing for our passage to Brazil. We needed to foresee every possible scenario because our lives depended on it. We estimated that it should take about thirty days from Dakar to Rio de Janeiro—at best maybe a few days less, and at worst… well, we preferred not to mull over a possible castaway scenario. We needed to have more than enough food, knowing that fishing was always an "iffy" option. We also planned on beaching *Cowabunga* for an annual hull cleaning. We couldn't afford to be slowed by barnacles and other sea creatures that had already begun to hitchhike in the past few weeks. Warm tropical waters encourage and facilitate the growth of sea creatures on a boat's hull, so they had been multiplying rapidly since reaching African latitudes.

There were no facilities to haul out a sailboat in Dakar, so by calculating the highest and lowest tides of the month, Michel homed in on the best days to complete this task. Purposely beaching a forty-two-foot sailboat is not an easy undertaking, and it was a project that I dreaded. Prior to beaching it, everything inside the boat had to be tied down, given the boat would rest at a 70°-80° angle for an entire day.

On the designated day, we were ready as the high tide reached its peak. We positioned *Cowabunga* parallel to the beach, at the highest point possible on the shore, with the keel barely touching the sand in the high water. Slowly the boat began to lean towards a resting place as the water was pulled from under it with the outgoing tide. Like a beached whale, *Cowabunga* was an awkward hulk.

We hurried to scrape, fit in some quick hull repairs, and add a coat of anti-fouling paint all before the tide came back in. There is always an anxious moment just before full flotation at high tide when we prayed that the boat would be fully righted. But physics did its job perfectly, and the incoming tide pushed on the bottom of the heavy keel, forcing *Cowabunga* into an upright position.

Despite being partially disappointed in Dakar, we still fully appreciated the experience. We learned something from every new place we visited, and while our stay in Dakar was not one of our fondest memories, there were some good times and amazing encounters. Almost one month into 1983, five months after we had left France, we lifted anchor to cross an ocean.

CHAPTER SEVEN

THIRTY DAYS

We set off across the expanse having exhausted all of our checklists, and still knowing there would be circumstances ahead we could never have prepared for.

One month in the middle of the ocean, with nothing but water in front, behind, and all around can be a long time…but it really wasn't. I remember that even after many days, we never found the 360° vastness of an ocean landscape to be boring. Yes, it was water, water, and more water, but it always evolved. It changed color, it varied in tempo, it altered its direction. The horizon would transform from smooth to choppy, from endless to enshrouded by clouds. Flying fish abruptly erupted through a rippled surface in large schools. Sudden pods of dolphins jumped around us and surfed in the wake of *Cowabunga*, or led the way just ahead of our bow. Sometimes at night, the inky water surrounding us would transform into an eerie field of hundreds of bioluminescent needlefish darting below the surface in an otherworldly tableau.

In their quest to cross the Atlantic, many cruisers start from the Canary Islands, sailing to the closest point in the West Indies, and eventually arriving in St. Barth, Antigua, Guadeloupe, Martinique, or Barbados. Such a crossing is about 2500 nautical miles and usually takes about three weeks with the trade winds. We wanted to take a passage less often pursued—crossing directly to South America. This trip would be about 2700 nautical miles and would take an extra week. We hoped to arrive in time for Carnaval in Rio. There wasn't any half-way stopping point, no place where we could quickly anchor, catch our breath, or rest up for a few days before continuing onward. Although we were going to cross some major shipping lanes, the chances of seeing many other boats were slim. It's a big ocean out there.

For our month at sea, we planned for everything we could think of. Along with food and water for two adults and two children, there were diapers to account for, baby bottles, "what-if" first aid items, etc. What if there were many windless days? What if there was a major mechanical malfunction? Or worse yet, what if we were to sink and have to seek refuge in the life raft? Consequently, we planned provisions for two or three months instead of just one.

Early on in our trip, I would think about our upcoming Atlantic crossing and wondered if we would get to the other side of that huge ocean safe and sound, and exactly to the spot we planned to land. As crazy as it seems, Michel only learned to use our sextant one week before our departure. Since there was no GPS in those days, we had no choice but to use an old-fashioned sextant for all our navigation. An early satellite navigation system was just beginning to make its debut for pleasure boats, but at $10,000, it was well beyond our means. Michel became very precise in his predictions within a day or two for our landfalls. He is a quick study, has a mathematician's knack for numbers, and he had proved his capability in using the sextant over the past six months, guiding us assuredly every inch of the way. There was never any doubt in my mind that we would arrive at Rio de Janeiro.

Navigation was an ongoing sore point between Michel and me because I didn't know the technical aspects of navigation. Manipulating the sextant, knowing how to do the calculations in figuring out our position, etc. I wasn't eager to learn. It didn't tempt my curiosity, and I kept putting it off, which irritated Michel. While I was an excellent crewmate, I was not a good sailor in the aspects of understanding how to properly set the sails. I didn't have a good feel for where the wind was coming from and how the sails should be set accordingly. I decided that we each had our strengths and weaknesses. Michel still thought I should be able to do his part, though, in case something was to happen. I had then, as I still do today, an extreme aversion to anything related to complicated mathematics, and computing sextant calculations fell into that category for me. I simply wasn't interested.

We set out during the Southern Hemisphere's summer after Michel had pored over the Pilot Charts. These are very elaborate ocean charts that indicate the prevailing winds and ocean currents for each month in minute detail, square-inch by square-inch. From these, Michel projected our route. We knew, however, that we would have to cross an area around the equator known as the doldrums, infamous for a total lack of wind that would most likely last for a few days. The doldrums were always present, shifting geographically north, south, east or west of the equator, depending on the season.

Up to this point, we thought we had become pretty intimately acquainted with ship life, but this month-long sail proved to be perfectly blissful. We were in harmony. Our daily routine was dictated by navigational duties, daily sextant sun sights, sail maneuvers, repairs, taking care of the boys, occasional fishing, and cooking.

Cooking on board was often an acrobatic endeavor. Even when sailing conditions were relatively tranquil, I still belted myself into the galley corner so I wouldn't get thrown about while working. Even when the waves and wind were calm and rocked systematically to a certain rhythm, I could easily get tossed to the other side of the boat with a hot pot of something in my hand. Michel had installed a standard, wide strap belt made of multi-purpose webbing which boxed me in and gave me something strong to lean against. I could even sit on it like on a swing and grab the counter, should the boat suddenly jerk. My body got used to anticipating the rock-and-roll motion, and I became quite adept a putting a liquid quiche into the oven under sail.

Michel often recounts our luck that we were able to eat well. The sea air and rocking movement of the boat made me hungry rather than sea sick. I remember the times of bad weather when Michel and the boys would go to sleep, hoping that it would be over when he woke up. I, on the other hand, would strategically place my body against the cupboard and gauge the swells to perfectly time opening a door for a snack so everything didn't tumble out. Besides, I was just too nervous to sleep! With a chocolate bar in hand, a few crackers, or whatever I could grab, I'd consistently poke my head outside, all-so-briefly, to monitor the situation.

Since we didn't have refrigeration on board, food and meals were planned accordingly. There was a whole separate strategy for keeping fruits and vegetables as fresh as possible. I bought them in various stages of readiness at the last minute: unripe and green, those that would ripen within a week-to-10-days, and those we could eat immediately. Cabbage eventually substituted for lettuce, and we grew our own sprouts on board.

I spent a lot of time in the days approaching the departure canning and preserving meats and fish, as well as preparing other dishes with my pressure cooker. With one "starter" yogurt, I was able to make yogurt throughout the whole trip. I was also able to make a basic cottage cheese and fromage blanc.

I had calculated how much bread I would need to make daily over a 30-day period, and made the same calculations for other items like eggs, milk, butter, fruit, vegetables, and other staples. My galley was well set up with plastic, airtight containers for rice, flour, pasta, etc. which kept the ingredients dry. One big advantage of launching from a third world country like Senegal was that many people didn't have refrigeration in their homes, making it easy to find items such as canned butter, canned heavy cream, and long-life milk in cartons. I even found some stew meat boxed in a vacuum-sealed brine solution. Almost as a joke, but to have on hand as a real last resort, we did have a few cans of Spam on board—the brunt of many cruiser's jokes.

As an added bonus, we carted along two live chickens which were designated to be our fresh Sunday dinners the second and third Sundays of our trip—and they were. Eggs were also always good fallback items if there wasn't much else to eat, and since I enjoy baking, I knew I would need quite a few. There were some handy strategies passed around in the boating community for keeping eggs fresh for several months without refrigeration. Some would dip their eggs for just an instant in boiling water; others would hard boil and pickle them. I subscribed to the Vaseline method, which consisted of coating each individual egg with a thin film of Vaseline. As an added precaution, we also turned each egg upside down once a week. The theory was that while the Vaseline prevented air from passing through the porous shell, inhibiting the egg from rotting, a traveling yoke couldn't settle on the shell and add to the egg's deterioration. We made space for 200 eggs to be stored during our crossing and were careful to be sure and turn them each week.

Any fish caught at sea was a bonus. If we somehow had the good fortune of capturing too much, there was certainly no throwing it overboard. On the few occasions when we did hook too much for just one meal, we immediately preserved the surplus through salting, dry-ing, and canning.

Early on during our passage, Michel, who is not a fisherman, set about learning how one should fish while sailing, especially in deep ocean waters. With thirty days of sea ahead of us, he had plenty of time to study the question.

The most important idea he came away with was from a book in our onboard library which discussed the need to create an environ-ment similar to a school of fish. To create such an effect from our deck, Michel devised a way of spreading out multiple fishing lines that trailed behind the boat. They were all different lengths and sported various lures and bait paraphernalia.

Sailboats such as ours carry at least one pole on deck, which is used for the downwind sail known as a spinnaker. The pole holds a bottom corner of the sail, jutting well out over the water to capture the most wind possible. As the course was charted, we found would probably have most days as a downwind trip, so we would be pushed by seasonal trade winds. Thus, in order to get the maximum speed out of our boat, we equipped *Cowabunga* with two spinnaker poles. This would allow us to hoist two downwind sails at the same time, on either side of the boat, putting us in a "wing-and-wing" position. With the two poles, we had a combined total of about thirty feet of potential fishing area to trail our lines from. This effectively gave the impression that we were a school of small fish, which then attracted bigger fish or at least we hoped that would be the case.

One afternoon, the wind slightly shifted, and we needed to change our angle downwind a bit. The fishing lines had been up for several days with no nibbles. They had become part of our on-deck landscape, blending into our routine. We hardly noticed them anymore. Michel shifted the angle of the wind vane, and in a domino effect, caused the trailing fishing lines in our wake to converge, all mixing and mingling until they became one big tangled web trailing behind us. No fish was going to be interested in that.

So Michel sat at the back of the boat for several days, untangling his "school of fish." After such an ordeal, I was of the opinion that the spinnaker pole technique was not ideal. Michel thought otherwise and wanted to give it another go. French men have a reputation for being difficult, and my husband is certainly French. Determined, Michel launched his school of fish apparatus several more times with new techniques, which only resulted in several more tangled messes. I thought it was comical and a huge waste of time, but he seemed to enjoy the test of his ingenuity. He finally began fishing with one or two lines at a time, and eventually did catch some fish.

Michel and I were strict about adhering to our scheduled four-hour watches. Typically, I took the midnight to 4:00 a.m. watch. I would nap from around 8:30 or 9:00 p.m. until midnight, and then take over from Michel. We tried variations on the watch schedule, every two or three hours, but these options didn't work for us. Admittedly, the fourth hour of the watch until 4:00 a.m. wasn't easy, but at least the person off-watch got a four-hour stint of sleep in. Two or three-hour sleeping periods were just not enough.

"Keeping watch" didn't necessarily mean keeping our eyes constantly fixed on the horizon. It meant keeping an eye on things in general: sounds that suddenly changed, the wind direction, the sails, the automatic wind vane pilot, the sleeping children, and also the horizon. Any red or green light in the distance would signal a boat: red lights on the port side, green lights on the starboard side. This international signal system is handy because depending on what color you see, you know from what angle the boat is approaching. A full-frontal view of a red and green light is not good, portending a head-on confrontation. We actually hoped to see a cargo ship or fishing trawler on occasion so we could initiate radio contact and confirm our position.

We didn't have to spend much time at the steering wheel thanks to our third crew member, the automatic wind vane pilot at the rear of the boat. Through an ingenious system of ropes rigged to the steering wheel, a wind vane sensor synchronized the rudder to the steering, and we were free to go about our day.

Sean and Brendan were always busy. Sean would play with his Lego blocks or what he called "mon bateau" (my boat) that we trailed in the water behind us. He would fish, draw, feed leftovers to the chickens who were perched in their cages on deck, and always, he talked. He asked questions about the sails, the sextant, the maps, and about fishing. He *loved* to fish and tweak ropes, or the "sheets," in the sailing parlance. He played well with Brendan, and they both spent a lot of time in our cockpit pool—a little inflatable bathtub we filled with seawater that they splashed around in.

Toys on board were a challenge. At first, both boys had a small toy chest with various cars, blocks, games, etc. But as they got older, we homed in on the Legos as our key toy. We didn't have room for big trucks, and many of the metallic toys quickly rusted. Sean and Brendan could easily piece parts together and bring to life their unique creations. We found ways to keep them organized and nicely stored away (in later years we devoted whole drawers to them), but this still didn't eliminate the occasional middle-of-the-night stomp on a sharp stray piece. By now Brendan was quite the crawler, and I was amused at how his body rolled with his environment. Having been on board since birth, the boat's movement was now part of him.

Conserving fresh water was a priority of daily life. We had an ample reserve of fresh water in our onboard water tanks, supplemented by additional jerrycans which we stored on deck. We used salt water as often as we could, mostly for showering and washing up dishes. We discovered that baby shampoo lathers up well with salt water, so that became our personal hygiene product of choice. Our soap and salt water showers were followed by a very stingy fresh water rinse, and we were clean every day crossing the Atlantic.

February third was a milestone for us—we hit the halfway point as we crossed the equator. We celebrated with champagne, having officially ventured into the Southern Hemisphere for the first time. On February eighteenth, we spotted land for the first time since leaving Africa: the Brazilian coast. As we grew closer, we were welcomed by huge manta rays jumping in the distance. It was quite spectacular, and as we sailed closer to them, they weaved in and out, gliding beneath us in the crystal turquoise water. At ten feet wide and forty-two feet long, our boat was dwarfed by these giants.

Having seen a few flashes from a lighthouse, Michel figured out we were about 300 nautical miles (about 345 miles) north of Rio de Janiero, and he announced that in another three days we should arrive. Around 1:00 a.m. on February twenty-first, I spotted a beacon: a very bright light that seemed to be in the sky, not on the coast. It looked more like an airplane, but much too bright and close. I was confused. As we approached and dawn shed the dark, the "sky light" proved to be the iconic statue of Christ, on the Corcovado. Michel and I were taken aback and emotional. After lifting anchor on January twenty-second, we slipped into Rio de Janeiro 30 days later, as Michel had perfectly predicted.

PART THREE

South America

CHAPTER EIGHT

ℛio!

ℛio de Janeiro! We did it! We crossed an ocean, we crossed the equator, we changed hemispheres. We landed on a new continent, in another culture, in another world. We were dumbfounded. We were jubilant!

Michel's landfall prediction was right on target, employing a navigation instrument used by ancient mariners. We were amazed—maybe dazed—to have crossed an ocean under our own power. It didn't sink in right away. Physically and mentally it was a strange feeling setting foot on land after 30 days at sea, and we had trouble adjusting to the stable ground. We had previously experienced smaller symptoms of "landsickness" after spending just a week at sea, but this time the feeling persisted for several days following our arrival.

Simple everyday things also seemed odd at first. Crossing a street proved a bit challenging; it took a few moments to register the meaning of a red light or a stop sign. Our brains worked in slow motion. A few times, we almost even regretted having arrived. Everyone seemed to be in a hurry, and everything felt rushed. All of humanity was crossing streets, boarding buses, going to school, buying groceries, busying themselves behind office windows… It was a bit overwhelming. What possessed us to make landfall in such a big city after one month of peaceful solitude? I found myself longing for some of those simple moments back out at sea.

But it was time to get our Brazilian adventure started. Contrary to our usual berthing practices of anchoring in a bay to avoid marina docking fees, this time we tied up in Rio's Marina da Gloria so we could more easily accomplish the entry formalities and get information on where we could anchor. We got initial instructions from the harbormaster's office. Michel took Sean with him to decipher the paper chase, which turned out to be a bureaucratic maze with layers of offices, passports, papers, and stamps.

They were gone all day! Usually, it took an hour or two, but they had to go to the police, followed by immigration, then customs, agriculture, the health department, and finally the Navy. It was the most cumbersome entry process we had ever dealt with. Compounding the aggravation was the diametrically opposed locations in the city ranging from north, south, east, and west of Rio, and one had to respect the order of which office to visit first. Adding to the difficulties was that Michel refused, as always, to cave into the awaited bribery. This, in combination with our poor knowledge of the city, the transport system, and the language, caused the whole day to prove as an exercise in human-wrought, useless complications.

At one point in Michel's trials, they even tried to turn away our children! Since the kids' visas were affixed to Michel's passport, the authorities deemed them invalid and stated that our boys would have to leave the country. Michel had to convince the Brazilian officials (while refusing to slip them the expected wad of bills) that our children were only three and one years old, and explain that he wasn't sure how they expected them to sail off by themselves. Thankfully, he was able to find Madame-the-head-of-something-or-other who recognized the insanity of the situation. With one thump of her powerful stamp, she rendered the problem a moot point.

As Michel shuffled through one step after the other, he was befriended by Dr. Bastos at the Public Health Service department who took a liking (or pity) to him. He accompanied my husband to some of the remaining offices as a translator, facilitating his understanding of some of the "technicalities." Dr. Bastos then accompanied Michel and Sean back to *Cowabunga* to verify our health records, and we were officially admitted to Brazil.

Then we plunged into Rio! It was hot, it was samba. It was very rich, it was very poor, and it was always about the beach. There were makeshift voodoo altars on crowded street corners, rampant crime and pickpockets. Cars and buses ran red lights to avoid the ever-present danger of robberies in stopped traffic. There were slums (favelas), unimaginable inflation, daily black-market money exchanges. The streets held a permanent odor of alcohol, which fueled the cars made in Brazil.

But Rio was also an abundance of lush, colorful, and new tropical fruits, pervasive at street-corner juice stands. It was Churrascaria restaurants, veritable orgy feasts of meat. It was the Caipirinha—the signature Brazilian cocktail. It was a place where children were kings. It was a kaleidoscope of dynamic contrasts, it was welcoming, it was relaxed, it was unpretentious, it was alive!

Brazil is most famous, of course, for its celebration of Carnaval. Not really knowing much about this Brazilian custom, we didn't think much about it until we arrived in Brazil. That's when we learned that it is the biggest and most elaborate celebration of the year throughout the country.

Originating from the Catholic pre-Lenten period of fun and feasting that heralds the onset of Lent's forty days of abstinence, the uniquely Brazilian samba dance and music define Brazil's celebration of Carnaval. Carnaval in Rio is perhaps the granddaddy festival of them all—an unbelievably huge, weeklong national revelry of parties, dancing, parades, and competition of the samba schools in Rio's specially-constructed Sambadromo. An outstanding feature of Brazilian culture, samba is not only their national hallmark, but it is singularly recognized throughout the world as the imprint of all things Brazilian. It is a revered pillar of their culture, a road to stardom for some, and a reason to live for others.

However, upon our arrival in February of 1983, we discovered that we had just missed it! This changed our plans for the year to come. We hadn't come this far not to see and experience this cultural phenomenon. We decided we would just have to stay in Brazil for the year, visas be damned.

We spent our first few weeks in a slip in the Marina da Gloria where I reveled in the easy access to unlimited running water, doing buckets and buckets of laundry. During our readjustment to docked life, our good friends from France, Philippe and Françoise, came to visit with their two young children. They brought a little bit of home to us while discovering and taking part in our lifestyle. However, it was also exhausting since they stayed with us on the boat, which necessitated a heavy amount of logistics to create living and sleeping quarters for additional bodies.

We eventually left the marina and anchored around the corner in the picturesque Guanabara Bay, where we had originally first sailed into Brazil under the gaze of Christ the Redeemer. The upscale and exclusive Iate Clube do Rio was located on the shore of the bay and was known to welcome foreign cruisers like us.

The club bid us avail ourselves of their services, free of charge. We had the best of both worlds then: a free anchorage and peaceful solitude in a beautiful setting, easy and quick access to the city and conveniences when we needed it, unlimited use of the yacht club showers and swimming pool. There was even a fully equipped ship-yard we were allowed to use, which we did at one point when we needed to haul out Cowabunga for the regular task of hull cleaning. The Iate Clube do Rio made a great effort in welcoming us cruisers. It was rather ironic that we—living a very basic, bare-bones life on a boat—would find ourselves occasionally hobnobbing with the for-tuned elite of Rio at the club bar or pool.

We met many new friends in Brazil, which always included genu-ine kindness and friendship, as well as frequent invitations. It was surprising to us that the invitations were for the four of us, children included. I mentioned before that children are kings in Brazil, and our newfound friends seemed perplexed when we questioned if our kids were invited. Why wouldn't they be? They were everywhere; they ruled the streets, they were excused, they were forgiven. Our boys were growing and changing and enjoyed being a part of all our outings. Sean learned how to swim and drive the Zodiac dinghy with the out-board engine, and Brendan took his first steps on the beach. They both also passed their childhood rites of passage with bouts of the chicken pox.

We also believe that thanks to the constant presence of our chil-dren, we were spared a lot of aggression and crime. Just about everyone we met in Rio had some story of a personal encounter, either with a holdup situation or with pickpockets. We were cautious to dress down when going into town, i.e., to forego jewelry and watches, wear simple cotton T-shirts and shorts, and keep money in our shoes or hidden under our clothes. Thankfully, we never experienced any personal attack.

Dr. Bastos became a regular visitor to our boat with his wife. They invited us out several times around Rio, as well as to their apartment in Copacabana. It soon became obvious that there was a wide class di-vide between the lifestyle of a public employee such as Dr. Bastos—

ensconced in the comfort of the visible luxury of Copacabana—and the poor slum dwellers situated in the favela, literally just around the street corner and up the hill from his home. We also found it curious that the poorest districts were located in what would be the upscale districts of any major city in France or the States. The favelas in Rio occupied key hilltop and hillside real estate with exceptional views. Yet this is where the cardboard huts and the tin-roofed cabanas hugged the unpaved, crime-ridden, muddy alleys.

Money in Rio in the 1980s was a joke. It was the era of hyperinflation, and the rate was over 100% when we were there. By the 1990s, the percentage was in the thousands! Prices in the grocery stores and shops changed every day. Consequently, we exchanged dollars for cruzeiros on a daily basis. The key was the unofficial black-market exchange rate. No one ever exchanged money in a bank or currency exchange office. The "official" black market rate was published every day in the newspaper, right next to the actual rate, and travel agencies were the "official" exchange spots. Perpetual lines snaked out of travel agency doors all day long, every day.

For us to stay in Brazil, we knew we would have to renew our visas every three months. As we approached the first three-month deadline, began to understand that in the spirit of the Brazilian way of life, we needed to, at times, fudge the truth a bit to make things more convenient.

Brazil's bureaucracy and economic oddities encouraged the Brazilians to be very inventive people. For example, since Brazil imposed hefty tariffs on imported goods at the time, highly prized international trademarked items were not available. Consequently, a "copycat" industry thrived. Well-known, internationally trademarked items were manufactured in Brazil and labeled *tipo* or "type." This meant the item was similar to its genuine counterpart, such as Swiss tipo cheese, Heinz tipo ketchup, etc. We took a cue from these entrepreneurs and de-cided to manufacture our own tipo tourist visas.

We discovered the trade of *carimbeiros,* which took place in little back alleys. Carimbeiros were rubber stamp makers who made "paid" stamps, "return to sender," and all manner of emblems of approval for visas, validations, certifications and the like. Bring in a photo or a sketch and a carimbeiro could turn it into a real, physical stamp over-night.

A fellow cruiser kindly let us make a photocopy of entry and exit visas he had acquired from the island of St. Helena in the South Atlantic Ocean. A British possession, it's known for having been the exile prison of Napoleon. Not many boats pass that way, and Brazilian au-thorities weren't likely to be familiar with the official stamps or paperwork of St. Helena. A carimbeiro created our St. Helena stamps in short order from the photocopies we supplied.

We then sailed along the southern Brazilian coast, lying low amongst some island anchorages as if we had left the country for a while. When we re-entered Brazil, we submitted our stamped pass-ports with a St. Helena entry and exit and gained fresh tourist visas for Brazil.

CHAPTER NINE

A Paradise Named Ilha Grande

In Brazil, we found paradise. Ilha Grande is an easy day sail, about sixty miles south of Rio de Janeiro. We wove our way through some of the 300-odd islands and magical anchorages with postcard-perfect, clear turquoise water, white powder beaches, and palm trees swaying in the breeze. Our experience there was rendered even more memorable thanks to our encounter and ensuing friendship with Peter, a local personality and the "King of Paradise."

Peter was a legend. A cruiser's conversation in general about Ilha Grande always included a reference to Peter. He was loved, boisterous, cantankerous, crusty, and unique. Known as "Peter at Peter's Place," he owned a corner of paradise—an idyllic refuge, dotted with palm trees on some acreage bordering Aroeira beach, in Abraão Bay. He was the king of his domain. Identifying himself as Austrian and rumored to have served in the German army in WWII, Peter let mystery waft about him. One didn't pry nor ask too many questions.

We learned about Peter in Rio while conversing with other cruisers, some of whom had spent time with him in his anchorage. Through
the ham radio airwaves, we connected with Peter, and he invited us to
anchor in his bay. Once anchored, the understanding was that we were
to come ashore and pay due respects, almost homage, to this man
whose generosity allowed the use and unique pleasure of basking in his
beautiful, calm, and secluded spot. In honor of his guests, Peter would
always fly their countries' respective flags. Thus, for us, both the
French and American flags rippled colorfully atop his flagpoles, clearly
visible from our vantage point on deck. The "sundowner" cocktail
hour was required by our eccentric host. Peter figured that if he
deemed a boat worthy of an invitation to his anchorage, he was to be
graced with his guests' presence for drinks at the end of the day. Not a
disagreeable contract to uphold.

The sundowner happy hours were usually lively international affairs since Peter's place was a regular hangout for passing boats. It was
always fascinating to learn everyone's story, and sometimes the cocktail hour morphed into an impromptu potluck dinner, well-anointed
with ample spirits and laughter. With a strong build and an imposing
stature of over six feet, Peter dominated the crowd with his hearty
laugh and polyglot ability, switching from fluent English, to German,
to Portuguese, and Spanish. He clearly enjoyed his paradise.

Peter made a point of saying that he didn't care for children. We
were up front about our two small ones, and he invited us nevertheless, giving us the benefit of the doubt. Apparently, Peter decided that
Sean and Brendan weren't too wild and crazy, and after a day or two,
he even exhibited a semblance of friendly tolerance for our two tykes.
He bid them play with his dearest pet pal, XoXa, a beautiful and very
tame, long-tailed gray monkey. Peter mentioned that XoXa was a type
of monkey prized by certain tribes for its unique babysitting ability and
that many families kept one as a nanny of sorts. One late afternoon

Sean and Brendan spent some time playing with XoXa on the grass in front of Peter's house, while several of us adults lounged and bantered during the sundowner cocktail hour. I don't know that I would have left the boys in XoXa's company as the sole babysitter, but for this brief time, the three of them kept each other happily occupied as XoXa would wrap and entwine her long arms around them.

Peter devoted a regular part of his day to communicate with the world via radio in his specially dedicated "radio shack" headquarters behind his house. It was his lifeline to the outside. I believe he relished his notoriety and the fact that his paradise had become a go-to spot on the cruising circuit. He led a simple and self-sufficient lifestyle and even ran a rudimentary solar power system that maintained a block of batteries to generate his own electricity.

Occasionally, however, there was a rift in paradise. Smack dab in the middle of all this picturesque tranquility, not too far from Peter's Place and hidden behind some hilly terrain, there lay a neighbor of ill repute: a notorious prison. Here, in Brazil's penal version of Alcatraz, dangerous criminals were incarcerated, and an occasional prison break occurred. We witnessed a recapture unfurl one morning on the beach.

My parents and sister were on board on this particular occasion. They had arrived from California several days earlier, and we whisked them away to experience this lifestyle with us. The prison authorities immediately alerted Peter, who prepared the handgun he kept by his bedside for just such an occurrence. We aborted our plans for dinner at a local cafe around the next bay. We'd have to travel there in our dinghy, and since escaped prisoners were known to steal or hijack any watercraft, we stayed on board for the evening and even hauled our dinghy up on deck for the night. Although we were all uneasy, concerned that we could cross paths with the escapees, there was nevertheless a nervous excitement since this was our first experience in such a situation. My father, who always thoroughly enjoyed re-counting such unusual personal anecdotes at dinner parties, came away fully armed with new and original fodder from this experience, ready to enthrall future dinner guests.

Peter insisted that we come ashore in the morning for a final fare-well and to stock up on some of his bananas before lifting anchor. We arose early with the sun already high and hot in the sky. There was a lot of activity on the beach, and from what we could see from our anchor point offshore, it looked like soldiers were milling around. It was, in fact, some of the prison guards who had caught some of the escapees. A promise to Peter was not to be broken, so off we ventured out in the dinghy anyway to say our final goodbyes. We landed on the beach amidst the unfolding drama, trying to keep our uneasiness in check as the guards held the prisoners prostrate and handcuffed at gun-point in the sand. It was hot, and there was no mercy for those miscreants. Intrigued by the suspense, we still maintained a healthy distance from the scene as it seemed there was still a missing prisoner or two, and other guards were continuing the search. Peter, unfazed, sauntered down to greet us, a load of homegrown bananas in hand. We all bid each other heartfelt goodbyes, and it was the last time we saw that paradise, but not Peter.

Things came full circle many years later when Peter looked us up in California with his then-new bride. Although still the strong, im-posing figure with his booming voice, Peter was beginning to show his age, slower in his gait, and a tad challenged with climbing stairs. My parents lived nearby, and seeing as Peter and my father had hit it off those many years ago (Peter had just the irreverent edge that tickled my father's fancy), my dad was thrilled to see Peter again. Peter seemed genuinely pleased to see Sean and Brendan again too, both grown boys by then.

As I write this now, we know that Peter has passed on, but he would be pleased to know that his paradise has been preserved as part of the Ilha Grande State Park. Peter founded his paradise, opened it to many of us, and now it continues to welcome others.

As we continued to wander Ilha Grande and its surrounding islands, we came upon the Guapo family. It was a happenstance encounter, and they swept us off our feet. As with other cruisers, we encountered along the way, *Guapo* was the name of their boat, otherwise known in civilian life as the Schurmanns: Heloisa, Vilfredo and their three young sons, Pierre, David, and Wilhem.

There was an instant bond between this Brazilian family and ours. They were exuberant about life, sailing, and their own project of sailing around the world. There didn't seem to be many long-term sailing Brazilian families (in fact, they were the first and only ones we met), and sailing around the world as a family was their dream. They peppered us with questions, and we traded thoughts, information, and tips over many dinner conversations.

We were impressed with how dynamic and energized our newfound friends were. They gave us a lot of local knowledge about sailing the Brazilian islands and accompanied us to an anchorage where we celebrated Sean's fourth birthday and spent Easter Sunday together. We even managed to host an Easter egg hunt, finding enough hiding places for candy-filled eggs for the five boys amongst the masts, shrouds, jugs, and poles of our two boats.

By the end of a few days together, they invited us to come visit them farther south in Florianopolis, where they lived. Since we had already flirted with the idea of heading down to Buenos Aires at some point to coordinate visa maneuvers, going to Florianopolis sounded like a possible winter option for a month or two.

Marking time in Florianopolis also put us within easy range of Uruguay and Argentina. Argentina had recently voted for its first democratically elected president since deposing the long-reigning military junta of the 1970s. If we timed it right, we could be present in the Plaza de Mayo for the historic inauguration day. What a motivator! It was decided.

By the end of May, the Southern Hemisphere summer was waning, and fall wasn't far off. One particular afternoon while we were under sail, we got our first taste of one of the transitory *frente frios* or cold fronts that roar up from Antarctica, which was a strange experience. In Europe, we were always used to bad weather coming out of the north or northwest, from the Arctic. Suddenly our light, pleasant breeze just died. The air was still, and we were totally becalmed, the sails flapping about. Off in the distance, a menacing black horizon approached, punctuated by lightning. Then the sky blackened, and abruptly, as if in a science fiction movie, our speed indicator eerily began clicking and logging erratically at a fast speed—yet we were dead in the water, not moving an inch.

Static-like crackling noises encircled us, like those that sometimes emanate from overhead power lines. We didn't dare touch anything. Then *bam*! A powerful southern blast of wind hit us out of nowhere like a hammer, and a violent electrical storm ensued. We had no choice but to let the wind chase us back to where we came from, retracing our course. We rode with it for about an hour and then it was over as suddenly as it had begun.

CHAPTER TEN

FLORIANOPOLIS

As we pushed south, we discovered that there was much more to Brazil than Rio. We took in the sights, history, folklore, and local characters of such places as the serene colonial anchorage of Ilhabela, and the industrial harbor of Santos. We took refuge from a storm in a charming hidden bay of Sao Francisco do Sul. Come the end of June, we set anchor in front of the Schurmann's home.

What a welcome! We didn't know what hit us. Like a tsunami, they swept us up in their arms and didn't let go until four months later. The Guapo family lived on the shore of a peaceful bay in a modern, grand home. They opened it to us without reserve. They arranged for us to have a more permanent long-term berth (free of charge) at their nearby yacht club, only about a half hour from their home. On weekends, they spirited us around to see the sights and always had a solution to a problem, such as where to find a reliable handyman. Constantly, the Guapos invited us for meals, insisted we use their washing machine, spend the night, and took us grocery shopping.

The *Guapos* insisted on babysitting for us on occasion so that we could have a rare date night—just the two of us. Heloisa even arranged for Sean to attend preschool at the same private school her children attended, also free of charge. His presence was welcomed as an opportunity to interact with a foreigner. Sean also learned to sail a bit in an Optimist, a tiny, single-handed and single-sail rigged sailboat, targeted as a good beginner boat for children.

Thanks to this, Sean quickly learned Portuguese and introduced us to a most amazing word, which was to become our own private catchphrase: *Bagunça!* Meaning "big mess," the school used it to designate a regular *hora da bagunça*, or the "hour of the big mess" where the kids could let loose. It was so perfect to describe so many situations; I loved it and took ownership of the word. I even named one of our cats "Bagunça" several years later.

Vilfredo, an economist, and Heloisa, the family organizer and project manager, were both huge personalities with non-stop, infectious "can do" spirits. No obstacle was too difficult to overcome, no goal too daunting to attain. They always followed through on their promises to us while they, themselves, were consumed by their project to leave and live on their sailboat, just as we had been a few years earlier.

We were also intrigued by their German last name, Schurmann. We learned that the south of Brazil was largely populated by German descendants, and not only were Germanic names quite common, but so were German-founded towns, the German language, and German customs. Vilfredo had his roots in this part of Brazil. Heloisa originally hailed from Rio de Janeiro, but she had spent much time in her early adult years in Miami as well, as evidenced by her flawless English.

Shortly after arriving while anchored in the bay, I had a rude awakening one morning when Brendan gave me a frightful scare. He was only 18 months old and had crawled out of his bunk, wearing his "bunny suit"—the full baby pajamas with the incorporated feet to guard against the cool nights. As I stood near the galley sink preparing the coffee, Brendan climbed right up the ladder to the exterior cockpit. I kept an eye on him since he wasn't too stable on his feet yet. He was outside on the deck, boxed in by the net that came up to his chin.

For safety purposes, we had a full net spreading the length of the boat on both sides to catch objects, or a child, should something or someone slip between the lines. Since we were at anchor, we placed an ice chest on the deck to allow more cabin space, unmindful of the danger of it. While preparing coffee, I glimpsed Brendan scrambling up the ice chest. I yelled for him to stop, but he was over the net and in the water with a big splash in two seconds flat!

The water was a green, glassy calm, and Brendan was sprawled out in his navy blue and red bunny suit. I couldn't say if he was floating or splashing about; that didn't register as I shot out to the deck and jumped over the side. In the split-second I splashed down, he was in the crook of my arm, and I tried to hold him up as high as possible while swimming around to the other side of the boat where we could climb up the ladder to the deck. It was all a blur, but thankfully he didn't have a lot of time to drink much water. The initial shock wore off quickly, and relief flooded as rapidly as panic had: it was done, over with, it had happened.

Once berthing arrangements were made for us at the Iate Clube do Florianopolis, we settled in, and it became our home for the next four months. We met and were adopted by the local characters and club members, and had a wonderful international community with them. We learned much about Argentina and Chile and their tormented histories from exiled expats, most notably Julio, known as "El Chileno," an exiled filmmaker from Chile. He had reinvented himself as a boat repair handyman for the yacht club and was gifted in canvas and sail repair work, stainless steel welding, and everything in between. His son, Alejandro, was a great companion for Sean, and they spent many an afternoon kicking around a soccer ball.

Then it started to rain, and rain. It was practically biblical; 40 days and 40 nights—or at least it seemed that long. When it rains every day for a month straight, what's another 10 days or so?

We had only been in Florianopolis for a month in July when the downpours began, inciting historic flooding in southern Brazil. Brazilian infrastructure wasn't sufficient to handle such a catastrophic situation, so the local powers-that-be launched a cry for help to the sailors and members of the yacht club. They asked if anyone with anything water-worthy be willing to volunteer for disaster relief and search and rescue operations. In the nearby town of Blumenau, the situation was desperate, and the only resources available were that of on-duty soldiers.

The yacht club organized quite an effort: a convoy with a trailer for the dinghies and a large collection of food and water. Michel joined the volunteers, packed up our inflatable Zodiac and little Seagull outboard engine, and left for five days.

Michel recounted total devastation in the flood zone. People were isolated on their rooftops and left to their own resources. Chickens and cows had sought refuge on a few hilltops. Initially, the yacht club team was charged with plucking people from rooftops and relocating them to higher ground. He remembers the military only served in a "disciplinary" capacity, making sure that people remained properly in line for food and water distribution.

Michel and other members of his team were frustrated with the ineffective soldiers, especially when emergency food supplies were running low. They wanted to salvage canned items from some of the devastated grocery stores since some of it could be distributed. Michel and a few others had brought some SCUBA diving gear, it would have been easy for them to retrieve some food. The soldiers, however, refused to allow it, lacking permission from their superiors.

Michel also told me of a heart-wrenching moment when a man was trying to cross the rushing current in his makeshift skiff to join an anxious woman awaiting him on the other side. The man set out on the water, and within seconds he overturned, never to resurface, and was just swept away. His companion was beside herself, and there was nothing anyone could do. Michel recalled feeling absolutely devastated, and entirely helpless.

Housed on the second floor of an electrical station, the rescue teams themselves would angle their boats up to the second-floor window, and crawl inside for the night. Their last day was heralded when they awoke one morning to find the dinghies hanging dry from the second floor. The water had receded. A month later, we drove through Blumenau. Debris and plastic bags were still hanging from the tall treetops. The deep red earth was saturated with water, and the car became caked in it. It was difficult to avoid tracking it everywhere. To this day, the flooding of 1983 remains one of the worst events in the annals of the area.

CHAPTER ELEVEN

Iguaçu and Fluid Frontiers

After our first six months in Brazil, our visas were about to expire again, and we had to deal with bureaucratic reality. It was time for us to cross a border, get our passports stamped as officially having left the country, and be allowed to re-enter Brazil with a clean slate. It was still too early in the season for us to sail down to Buenos Aires, and since Florianopolis was within a reasonable reach of Paraguay, it was the most accessible border to enter and leave Brazil for a day. Iguaçu Falls was right on our projected path.

Off we went in a rented VW Beetle, loaded up with diapers for Brendan and warm clothes for us since the southern hemisphere was starting its transitional, fickle spring weather. Heading north from Florianopolis to Curitiba, and finally, west to the town of Foz do Iguaçu, we plied some backroads and byways of Brazil's southern backcountry. I love road trips. They're the best way to discover the soul of a place and its people, and we were well-served on this adventure.

It was a drive back in time as we carved our way through the lush semi-tropical interior of the country. Very few roads were paved, and we encountered considerable poverty. Distant and isolated from the more prosperous coastal cities, the underdevelopment and neglect were starkly obvious as we drove by primitive wooden shacks clinging to muddy hillsides that lacked indoor plumbing and other modern conveniences.

The heavy German influence on the population was very different from the variety of ethnicities we became accustomed to in Rio. In one particular encounter, we were waiting in line to take a primitive ferry boat to cross a river. It was a crude, wooden raft-like barge that could only carry a handful of cars and pedestrians at a time. A very pregnant blond-haired woman cradled an infant in her arms and was surrounded by several equally blonde-haired and dirty, disheveled children who kicked their bare feet through the mud. It was a scene reminiscent of a backwoods hinterland, not the paradise we associated with Brazil. Elsewhere, we passed farmers on the road in wooden carts while others plowed their fields with oxen and hand plows—in 1983!

We made it to Foz do Iguaçu, approximately 600 miles northwest of Florianopolis, and were not disappointed with the falls. Here, the Iguaçu and Parana rivers converge in a spectacular explosion of cascading walls of water. Forming a panoramic marvel of deafening, crashing water and churning foam, it was like being in the heart of an Imax movie; a non-stop live action screen towering above our craning necks. There was so much mist from all the spray that we were immediately soaked.

Never having been to Niagara Falls myself, Michel, who had, affirmed that they couldn't compare with Iguaçu. Other accounts I have read since also insist that Iguaçu Falls should rank as perhaps the most majestic and amazing of the natural wonders of the world, and even most recently as 2011 the falls were ranked the top spot in the Lonely

Planet's Reader's Picks of the New Seven Natural Wonders of the World.

With our tourism cravings fulfilled, it was time to concentrate on the business at hand and our initial reason for the trip in the first place. We drove to the border of Paraguay at the Friendship Bridge that crosses the Rio Parana, parked the car, and loaded Brendan papoose-style into his baby backpack. With some trepidation, the four of us left Brazil on foot. We hoped nothing would go wrong, and we could get back into Brazil. We had left our whole life with *Cowabunga,* back in Florianopolis.

Border towns, of course, are not always the best example of what a country has to offer, and the scene at the bridge checkpoint was probably not Paraguay at its best, although it was comical. At the time, Paraguay was governed by the well-entrenched dictator, General Stroessner, one of the last holdouts of the breed of South American dictators of that era. This innocuous, far-flung outpost apparently seemed to be a popular spot for wanna-be secret government agents to show off their undercover skills.

Probably well over half of the people milling around were gentlemen "disguised" in stereotypical spy garb: trench coats, dark slacks, shiny black shoes, sunglasses, slicked down black hair, 60s era hats, Latin mustaches. They busied themselves by indulging in dramatic and indiscriminate car and body searches. The icing on the cake was a tall military officer surveying the scene from his regal perch atop a large planter. Framed by his bright green uniform, a shiny black patent-leather brimmed cap, and aviator sunglasses, he drew lengthy breaths from his long cigarette. He struck quite a haughty pose as a native man furiously shined his already high-gloss black boots. The portrait was too tempting to ignore, and we really wanted a snapshot of this officer. Sensing, however, that this might be ill-advised given the surrounding scene, Michel approached the officer to ask his permission. Our response was a curt "No."

Amusement aside, we made our way into the border office where our passports were stamped, admitting us into Paraguay. This formality was sufficient for Michel and the boys to re-enter Brazil under their French passports. However, for me as an American, I needed an additional visa, so we trekked further into the gritty border town of Puerto Stroessner, seeking the U.S. Consulate. The town was teeming with street life as a multitude of duty-free hovels leaned on each other. Indigenous locals hawked wares and trinkets dangling from their backs and hands, odors abounded from food stalls, and we dodged what we could of the dirty sidewalks and gutters.

It had been a full day before we re-entered Brazil at Foz do Iguaçu that evening, hitting the road again. We relished the trip, yet were eager to be back on the boat, heading to our next port.

CHAPTER TWELVE

ℋEADING ℒOUTH

We left Florianopolis on November first, a calm spring morning, alongside our friends Yves and Isabelle on the French sailboat, *Le Geko*. They had recently sailed into the harbor, and we all decided to head south together for a bit of the journey. We anticipated only being a week or so at sea, and voilà, we'd be in a whole new world: Argentina.

We bid goodbye to the Guapos. Our strong friendship would continue to be a running thread in our travels.

They went on to accomplish great things. They completed three sailing tours around the world with three different boats (*Guapo*, *Aysso*, and *Kat*), and created books and documentaries about their exploits. They are now celebrities in Brazil as the first Brazilian family to have accomplished a circumnavigation. They still sail today, and while they are the Familia Schurmann to the world, they are always the Guapo Family to us, embodying generosity, friendship, and an immense spirit of "can-do."

Buenos Aires has owned such a tortured history. From the political upheaval in the 1950s, wrought by the power couple Juan and Evita

Peron, to the horror of the military junta of the 1970s. I remembered images from nightly TV news reports of the "Madres de Mayo"—the Mothers of May of the Plaza de Mayo—with their large banners displaying their *desaparecidos*, or their "disappeared" children.

December 10, 1983, was to be inauguration day, and the installation of Raoul Alfonsín, the first democratically elected president of Argentina. This would grandly mark the end of a horrific era of rampant killing and torture that had paraded nightly across our televisions back in France. We wanted to be present in the famous Plaza de Mayo for this momentous celebration. Since the event coincided with the end of our latest Brazilian visa, it was the perfect juncture and a once-in-a-lifetime opportunity.

Aside from our attraction to Buenos Aires, we were also drawn to the southern part of South America for the sailing lore and legends prompted. There are many tales of souls who braved the "Roaring 40s" latitudes and some who continued on around Cape Horn. It was daunting knowing that we were going to cross into those same latitudes, so we did a lot of good reading about the most ideal times of year to venture south while considering the weather patterns, weather histories, and Pilot Chart wind tendencies. Well, I'll have to be honest here: it is a lot to say "we," and I must give credit where credit is due. "We" was essentially Michel, him being the navigator.

The infamous *pamperos*, erratic, violent evening summer thunderstorms, were a worry for us. These squalls can hit boats with an incredible tornado-like force and can last for days. For better or worse, you can see them approaching in the distance. The best you can do is "batten down the hatches": take down the sails, secure everything you can, prepare psychologically, and just wait for it to pass. We left during November, which we calculated would have the lowest possibility of our having to deal with a pampero.

Barely out of Florianopolis, we were tossed around violently—a cork on a wild sea of foam, with 50 knots of wind. As the sea grew more frenzied, I became alarmed, and I seriously wondered if *Cowabunga* was going to pull us through intact. This wasn't part of the dream scenario we had sketched out for our vagabond life; this was hell. It hit me that we were also not far from the infamous Roaring 40s. Despite our determination to avoid such bad weather, there we were, confounded, and in the midst of a maelstrom.

It was petrifying. Huge waves crashed on the deck, and there were constant thumps against the hull as the boat constantly heaved against the wall of the sea. Would the boat hold up? Would we lose the mast, or worse, the stabilizing keel? What if we did a 360°, which meant *Cowabunga* would completely roll over? And the boys... So many "what-ifs" raged in my head. We had been in radio contact with *Le Geko,* and they confirmed that they were also in the storm. Having contact with them was comforting, both to not be "alone" and to know that they were all right. But then communication with them went dead. We couldn't get a response, and our fear heightened.

It was my turn at the helm. Michel had already reduced the sail area quite a bit, having taken reefs, or folds, in the main and mizzen sails. He had also rolled up our large front-end roller furling sail, or genoa, to the size of a storm jib (a sail characterized as "handkerchief-sized") meant to act as a stabilizer in bad weather. Despite these measures, I was still having a difficult time handling the wheel, trying to resist the force of the waves while surfing through the churn. Michel was surveying the waves breaking on our stern when he suddenly said:

"That's it. On s'arrête. Time to stop." He surprised me with his absolute firmness and certitude. It must have been bad.

Since I had my back to the scene, I didn't see what he saw: a huge breaking wave, taller than the boat and about collapse on us. It could have put us briefly under water or caused us to capsize. In such a case, we would have undoubtedly sustained a lot of damage, or even the unthinkable, had to abandon ship. "Stopping" the boat, however, didn't mean just put on the brakes. It meant we needed to stop trying to make any meaningful headway, and just "heave to." We would simply stop fighting the elements, and attempt to stay more or less in the same geographical area. To accomplish this, we reined all the sails in except for the storm jib. The boat reacts like a cork in this configuration, flowing with the waves and current, rather than bucking the elements as it would be trying to capture the wind for propulsion.

Once all this maneuvering was done, there wasn't much else we could do except stay down below and wait for it all to blow over. Sean and Brendan had been down below during all of this were actually having a great time. They made a fort in the main cabin and were enjoying being tossed about from one side of the cabin to the other. They thought it was great fun. Not wanting to reveal to them how scared we were, Michel played the '60s French rock song, *Les Elucubrations* as loudly as possible, drowning out the outside roar, and got the kids to sing along. The main refrain in the song finishes with an emphatic "oh yeah," only in French it comes out more like "oh yé." To this day, it is referred to in our family as the "Oh Yé" song. That day it kept us distracted from what was happening outside—and kept us sane.

The morning after was calm and peaceful, but the deck of *Cowabunga* had been wiped clean. Whatever hadn't been tied down was long gone—washed overboard—and for what remained, much of it was damaged. One of our spinnaker poles, which had been lashed to the side of our foredeck, had been bent out of shape by the waves. It was mind boggling to see what an enraged sea can do.

We were heartbroken to see that the most significant damage was to our autopilot or wind vane, which was, importantly, the third crewmember on board. It stayed in sync with the sails, the helm, and the rudder, steering the boat by itself, simply under wind power—no batteries needed.

Michel was able to determine that a crucial part had broken, causing vital parts to fall into the sea. Michel is quite the handyman, good at jury-rigging things, but this was beyond any solution he could manage without new parts. We were 100 miles out to sea and following a coastline with no viable ports for repairs. The nearest feasible harbor was at least a week's sail away. We had no choice but to continue without our third crew member, and the unknowns of how we would do it were worrisome.

Handling the boat between the two of us wasn't the problem. We had already been doing that for several years. But simultaneously manning the helm, maneuvering the boat, keeping watch, cooking, and caring for two small children was new. Whoever was on duty at the helm couldn't rest once that watch was over. The boys would need their meals or snacks, or diaper changed. Dinner had to be made, or the daily bread to be kneaded and baked. We were exhausted after the storm, not having slept for over twenty-four hours, and now we were looking at least another five or six days with little sleep until landfall.

We had originally targeted our arrival in Uruguay to be the port of Montevideo, just inside the mouth of the Rio de la Plata. We scoured the map for a quick alternative solution. The nearest safe harbor we could reach would be La Paloma, still north of the Rio de la Plata, but a decent place to rest and get our wits about us. One of the many lessons we learned while sailing—or at least one that Neptune actively tried to teach us—was patience. Patience when the wind wasn't there, patience when all hell broke loose, patience when the rain wouldn't let up, patience when everything broke, patience when waiting for parts, patience with customs and immigration formalities. Another lesson in patience was certainly in store for us following that tempest.

CHAPTER THIRTEEN

URUGUAY

Sean and Brendan weren't able to comprehend that we were just too tired to properly take care of them as we limped along after the storm. We simply had to make do and take it slow. Once it settled in our minds that we would be moving slow for a week and that we had no choice, we accepted it. We were lucky that the weather held out for those next few days, and when we just couldn't see straight anymore, we took advantage of some windless periods, putting the boat once again into a "heave-to" position, and took turns napping. It was such a luxury to sleep two or three hours straight through.

Through my cloud of exhaustion, I suddenly realized how far south below the equator we had come when I happened to notice some odd splashing alongside the boat. It was much too small for a dolphin, and a fish wouldn't be on top of the water. Then I saw that it was a penguin—the first time I had seen one outside of a zoo!

We finally glided into La Paloma early one peaceful morning. *Cowabunga* was intact; no one would guess what we had lived through over the past week. Just as we came around the breakwater, we spied *Le Geko*. We were thrilled to see them, but then saw why we had been unable to reach them on any radio frequency: our damage was minimal compared to theirs. They had suffered a knockdown, a situation sailors have nightmares about. Waves can overpower a boat, completely knocking it down on its side—mast and all. It can be forced into the water or even slightly under. The spreaders were contorted, their spinnaker pole was bent in half, their navigation night-running lights were gone (indicated by the remains of spindly connection cords which swung loosely about). The mizzen boom was broken, and sails were ripped. It looked like a ghost ship. It seems they were still under sail and the main hatch had been open when the devastating wave hit. The interior had flooded, destroying all their electronic equipment and wreaking considerable water damage throughout.

We were overjoyed to see them, and that they had made it through the storm. We banged madly on their hull, waking them up once we had tied up alongside. We were taken aback by the two ghostly figures that emerged. Isabelle's long blonde hair was one huge tangled rat's nest, and Yves had quite a black eye and a noticeable limp. He had been thrown to the ceiling when they were hit, and apart from his injury, the dent and crack in the ceiling were proof. We then realized how lucky we were and how close to a catastrophe we could have come if we hadn't hove-to when we did.

We all stayed in La Paloma for almost two weeks, sleeping, regaining our composure, determining what parts we needed for the wind vane pilot, repairing what we could, and planning our next steps. Some very kind local fishermen brought us fried fish and steaks for dinner and even invited us to their homes for hot showers. The only way to get the parts we needed, it turned out, would be to have them delivered to Montevideo. We decided to make the trip to Montevideo in short spurts, to minimize our sailing days without the wind vane autopilot. Thus, our next port of call was Punte Del Este, an up-and-coming, trendy South American summer beach resort. *Le Geko* wasn't in ideal operating condition, so we left together. Since our electronic equipment was still operational, they leaned on us for navigational assistance.

We didn't stay long in Punte Del Este since we were eager to get to Montevideo, and we weren't terribly interested in this Miami-style ambiance. There was quite a bit of rain while we were there, and Michel went into town to run some errands after it finally stopped. He happened upon a wall that was covered with garden snails, ordinary things to anyone walking by. But to a Frenchman, these were escargots! He couldn't let this opportunity pass and hurried back to the boat for a bucket. Isabelle was also keen on collecting them.

Uruguay was still a military dictatorship at this time, so anything at all suspicious—such as two adults and a little boy enthusiastically plucking snails off a wall—would most assuredly attract the attention of two nearby soldiers, which it did. They demanded to see their passports, then a wave of understanding washed over their faces. Ah, they are French. Of course! Snails! No more explanation needed. Our escargots turned out to be an unexpected bonus, providing us with a lighter moment and a culinary delight.

Pulling into the harbor of Montevideo not only gave us the opportunity to finally order the needed parts from the U.S., but we also learned that we could order these parts under the auspices of special Uruguayan import tax advantages, reserved for visiting foreign yachts. Furthermore, at this physical location, we gained a firm foothold in the Rio de la Plata, now only being a day's sail from Buenos Aires.

Through Yves and his ham radio contacts, we met Georges, Guillermo, Andres, and a host of Franco-Uruguayans and French expats, all of whom facilitated our parts orders, repair contacts, and gave us a grand welcome to their corner of the world. The timing worked out equally well in that the last of the Antarctic-wrought cold fronts barreled through while we were snuggled at the dock.

Uruguayans were only too aware of neighboring Argentina's return to democratic rule. Only the Rio de la Plata separated the two counties, and cracks in Uruguay's military rule were beginning to show. There were rumors that a large street protest was imminent in downtown Montevideo. Although we both wanted to go and take Sean and Brendan, we decided that it would be prudent if only Michel ventured out to the event, just in case tempers flared. Michel reported that it was extremely peaceful. It was a most civilized and non-confrontational gathering of men, women, children, and families, some even with babies in strollers. They paraded en masse down the streets, waving banners and employing the signature South American protest soundtrack: banging pots and pans.

Soon thereafter, our parts arrived, the repairs were made, and we cast off and captured the upriver tide of the mighty, muddy Rio de la Plata. We would make good on our promise to witness history in Buenos Aires.

CHAPTER FOURTEEN

BUENOS AIRES, ARGENTINA

We had sailed overnight up the Rio de la Plata from Montevideo, taking care to navigate well within the buoy-lit channel to avoid the shallow areas. After making our initial entry in Argentina at the harbor office in Buenos Aires, we continued a few more miles into the harbor of San Ysidro. Now it was *the* day: December tenth!

This was Argentina's day in the sun, and we were there—witnesses to this once-in-a-lifetime historical event. All of South America was aflame with excitement and anticipation of this truly momentous occasion. As the fall of the Berlin Wall was to precede Eastern Europe's tumble from Communism, Argentina was to be the first country of our era's spate of South American dictatorships to entirely shed its legacy of military control. It proved to be the beginning of a chain reaction, with authoritarian regimes in Chile, Uruguay, Paraguay, and Bolivia toppling later.

Buenos Aires at the apex of its summer season and it was hot. Really hot. Thousands upon thousands of people were giddy, milling around, waiting anxiously in the Plaza de Mayo, which is the central hub and heart of Buenos Aires. Excitement punctuated the air. The Madres de la Plaza de Mayo were there, ever faithful to their post. I was awestruck to see these determined mothers and grandmothers brandishing their famous banners and poster photos of their children.

The crowd stood shoulder-to-shoulder, a mass of shimmering colors, filling the Plaza as far as you could see. The people fanned out below the balcony of the famed presidential palace, the anchor of the Plaza, the Casa Rosada. An expansive square with origins dating back to the late 1500s, the Plaza de Mayo is framed by Neo Classical and Italianate architecture—majestic government buildings, monuments, and a cathedral. A wave of energy began to travel through the crowd as Raoul Alfonsin's black limousine weaved toward the balcony.

Little black and red flags emblazoned with "Alfonsin" shook in the air above the crowd to the rhythm of a universal chant, "Alfonsin! Alfonsin!" I still laugh when recalling this scene because Brendan, who was not quite two years old and perched on Michel's shoulders, surveyed the spectacle, taking it all in. For a long time after that day, he thought "Alfonsin" meant "flag."

The new president gave a rousing speech from the same famed balcony where Juan and Evita Peron had rallied the faithful and launched their movement for the people over thirty years before. The crowd was delirious, and deafening as they clapped, shouted, cheered, blew horns, and beat drums. Incessant confetti rained down all afternoon from the surrounding buildings, turning the entire plaza snow white.

Representatives from countries the world over came to lend their support, enthusiasm, and encouragement to Argentina. We spotted the U.S. Vice President at the time, George Bush senior, among the many dignitaries in their country-flagged limousines. Celebrations throughout the city lasted all day and into the night, and we eventually retreated to *Cowabunga*, savoring our memories of the day.

Buenos Aires sported a European flair that resonated from its architecture, sidewalk cafés, city bustle, and even the physical traits of the people. We were impassioned by their descriptions of unique geographical riches and splendors such as the far reaches of Patagonia, the *pampas*, the Andes, the vineyards, the ski resorts, and the powerful Rio de la Plata. Also, the generosity of this people put us to shame. Since we had come on our small sailboat from so far away, we were labeled *ultramar* sailors from "across the sea," and in their minds, this merited us a royal treatment. Our one-month stay in the yacht club included full use of the facilities, and a haul-out in their shipyard, entirely free of charge. The yacht club's administration even appointed a host at our disposal to drive us into the city, show us around, and be available for any information or errands we may need. There were several other foreign cruising boats there at the same time, and they were welcomed in the same manner.

During our time there, we learned about the Argentinian passion for meat and feasted with them at some of their legendary *asados*—spectacular, overindulgent barbecue banquets that put our American hamburger-grilling get-togethers to shame. Through happenstance encounters with some locals, we learned about their political passions and the journey that brought their country to their recent democratic victory. We also learned about their rich multicultural past, wrought from a mixture of Italians, Spanish, French, and Germans, along with the more mestizo Spanish-Amerindian populations of South American countries. Many Argentinians we met were overwhelmingly well-educated, often bi- or multilingual, and admirably cultured. Well-versed in world history and current world events, they were a far cry from the illiterate, easily-duped populace my ill-informed prejudice had led me to believe.

After seeing the native land of Che Guevara, Michel and I began to understand why this country and other South American countries resented the United States. I realized that the short, cryptic commentary of world events on the American evening news hadn't told the full story. Edited footage was broadcast to illustrate certain stories or angles, and as a teenager then, I was too selfishly engaged in my world to pay attention to or dig deeper for the real story. Even though our newfound friends and acquaintances joyfully welcomed our family, they did not hold much love for the American government. The U.S. had long been meddling in South American affairs. Everything from interference in covert operations for regime changes, to mandates dictated by American multinational corporations. South America can't— and never will be—just a southern version of us from the north. We really came to realize that their needs, priorities, and desires cannot be compared to ours.

We celebrated Christmas in Buenos Aires, and then hauled the boat out at the shipyard for the annual hull maintenance work. Constrained by our self-imposed timeline to return to Brazil by February for Carnaval, our remaining time passed quickly, and we deeply regretted having to leave. We were frustrated, feeling that we had barely scratched the surface of what there was to learn and see in Argentina. We prepared to lift anchor, but we still had one more detail to tend to before bidding our final farewell to Buenos Aires.

One year earlier, we had a midnight radio exchange with an Argentinian freighter during our transatlantic crossing. "American ship, American ship, calling American ship," came through on the VHF radio, on Channel 16. Channel 16 on the VHF radio is an open channel, something like the telephone party lines of days gone by, or today's open chat rooms online. This cargo contact proved to be surprising. The Argentinian freighter, *Neuquén II*, was returning to Buenos Aires from Le Havre, France. Some of the *Neuquén II* crew had overheard our conversations between two other cargoes earlier in the evening, and they were intrigued that I, a woman, was on the high seas. They were even more astonished to learn that we were a family on a small sailboat.

After a good hour of lighthearted banter with some American bashing and macho entreaties for me to "throw Michel overboard" and join them, the captain, Enrique Carlos Marthi, then commandeered the microphone. He insisted that if we were ever to sail to Buenos Aires, we must look him up, and he gave us his address and phone number. At the time Buenos Aires hadn't figured into our plans yet, but since our plans unfurled the way they did, we thought we might as well try to find him before we left.

I had written Captain Marthi earlier when we knew we would be heading south from Brazil. He replied rather quickly, saying that he remembered us and that as far as he knew his ship should be in their home port of Buenos Aires for Christmas. However, as we kept tabs on the *Neuquén II*'s whereabouts during December, we found out that they had been held up in Houston and wouldn't be back in Buenos Aires until the first week of January. Since we were planning on leaving by then, we would probably miss them.

On our departure day, January fourth, we were stuck in the mud at the dock at the San Ysidro Yacht Club. Such was our misfortune when a strong north wind kept the water level quite low. The following day, however, we were able to scoot out to the main harbor of Buenos Aires. After completing our exit paperwork with the passport office, and we were off.

As we skirted the freighters in the industrial harbor on our way out, we regretted not having been able to meet up Captain Marthi. But as luck would have it, we rounded the bend, and voilà! Rising like a monolith smack dab in front of our bow was none other than the stern of the *Neuquén II*.

Angling *Cowabunga* to come about, we re-anchored, and Michel rowed ashore to make the phone call. The timing couldn't have been more perfect. Captain Marthi was not only home, but that very evening his whole family was gathering to celebrate his birthday with an elaborate Argentinian asado. He insisted we come, and that they would pick us up at the harbor.

We were giddy; it was like going on a blind date. We were finally going to put faces to the midnight voices from one year earlier. Welcomed in the grandest of manners at his home, Captain Marthi treated us to a full Argentinian menu of grilled sausages, steaks, and varied items that just kept multiplying off their state-of-the-art Argentinian barbecue. Any home that deemed itself worthy of hosting a backyard asado wouldn't be caught dead without one of these industrial wonders. Thanks to various levers, chains, and pulleys, the grill could be raised or lowered to just the right settings of flame and heat. Captain Marthi, along with his family, was most gracious and generous, welcoming us into their fold. We were honored by his invitation, and between our broken Spanish and his respectable English, we peppered each other with questions about Argentina and mutual travels across the seas. After that exhilarating day, we trekked back to *Cowabunga* for one last night in Buenos Aires, frustrated once more that we had to leave. Our month there was much too short.

CHAPTER FIFTEEN

Goodbye Rio, Hello Beyond

Heading out on the muddy Rio de la Plata to the mouth of the South Atlantic Ocean was tedious, and our tempers flared. With the wind on the nose, onboard conditions were uncomfortable. Since the river was shallow, the wind whipped the water up into short choppy waves that jumped on deck, splashing into the main cabin. Salt water on the couch, cushions, and other soft surfaces would never properly dry out since the salt maintained a pervasive, annoyingly clammy consistency in the fabric. To avoid clammy cushions, we had to keep all the hatches closed tight, and since it was very hot outside, it was stifling inside.

Adding to the bad mood mix, Michel had decided (again) to quit smoking, and consequently, we left Buenos Aires without any cigarettes on board. His occasional stop-and-go attempts to quit over the years had been unsuccessful, and by the fourth day of these conditions, he was insufferable. Pulling into Punte del Este at the mouth of the river for a rest—and to buy cigarettes—I decided that as much as I hated him smoking, it was preferable at this point to ease some of the reigning tension.

Finally, ten days later, we were back in Brazil with a clean slate for our tourist visas. We returned to Florianopolis for a brief visit with our friends, Familia Guapo, and then headed back up to Rio for the famous Carnaval.

Barely twenty-four hours after leaving Florianopolis, we had to turn back. A sudden catastrophic failure of our genoa roller furling system sent us in a limping retreat to the harbor. It was a calm, warm, sunny day and we were gliding along quite nicely when a sudden, loud *crack* came from the forestay. The forestay is the main cable that leads from the top of the mast down to the front end of the boat, and the front sail—or genoa in our case—is hoisted along this cable. The cable was housed within a long metal tube which allowed us to roll the sail in or out to increase or decrease its area. A drum on the bottom of the tube was the actual device that turned the tube, and the advantage of this system was that we didn't have to physically lower or hoist a different sail to fit wind changes.

The whole system—the forestay with the roller furl assembly, including the bottom drum and the genoa under full sail—began swinging around wildly, tethered only at the top of the mast like one giant pendulum. Michel quickly took evasive action by putting us into a heave-to position, minimizing our movement and the swinging around of this heavy, dangerous equipment. He was finally able to catch hold of the unwieldy drum and immobilize it.

Once the drum had stopped swinging, we needed to get the sail down since it was creating a tremendous drag and awkward listing of the boat. It had also been ripped in several spots by the runaway drum. The only choice was to release the halyard (the cable for hoisting the sail along the tube) that held the sail at the top of the mast, while we both attempted to gather the sail and tubes onto the deck as it descended. The huge mass of full sail, weighed down with the metal roller tubes, just crashed into the water. The sinking, curling mass entangled itself under the keel.

In its normal state, all this equipment was heavy. But now underwater and wet, it was like trying to hoist up a whale with our bare hands. We couldn't afford to just cut it all away, let it sink, and buy new equipment. We had no choice but to try and save it all. We spent hours hoisting all of this, inch-by-agonizing-inch, back onto the deck. It was an absolute nightmare. After jury-rigging a system with some other cables and some spare sails, we were back on our way to Florianopolis a good eight hours later.

Once again, the sea taught us a new level of patience. Installing new parts, repairing the rigging, and sewing became our priority. But even though this interrupted our plans, we weren't too distraught. After ten additional days, we bid farewell to Florianopolis once again, and it was onward to Rio.

Carnaval! Full of vivacity, frenetic street festivals, and unforgettable evenings of theatrical extravagance. We romped with Sean and Brendan amidst euphoric crowds to the infectious beat of samba throughout Rio's teeming streets. The boys were wide-eyed and all smiles as we melded into the musical melee. The samba beat had its own heart and soul, and the festivities culminated each night with a breathtaking, glittery parade of the top twelve competing samba schools. With over 3,000 members each, the spectacle lasted from dusk to dawn as nonstop dancers, singers, and musicians gyrated and strutted in sumptuous and ornate costumes to each school's original music, all accompanied by elaborate floats. We were not disappointed to have prolonged our year in Brazil.

After Carnaval and some time spent port-hopping through neighboring cities, we realized that Rio had been our rallying point for well over a year, and now it was time to move on. During one of our last weeks, we went back briefly to the Marina da Gloria to fill up on water and tend to other chores for our departure. There, we met a French couple, Patrick and Sylvie, as they had spied our French flag from the docks. Residents of Australia, they were passing through Rio on vacation.

Sometimes things just click with certain people, and so it was with Patrick and Sylvie. After an exchange of customary greetings and some polite conversation, we invited them onboard for a beer, which stretched into an impromptu dinner, and then several more dinners in the days that followed. We felt as if they had been our best friends for years. They were easy going, had a great rapport with Sean and Brendan, a good sense of humor, and perhaps the icing on the cake was that they had a restaurant back home in Australia. Sylvie knew how to make bread and pizza dough! After a year and a half of trying to perfect my bread-making skills, I still only had occasional successes. Sylvie showed me her simple tricks in just a few minutes, and the mystery was solved.

We invited Patrick and Sylvie to travel with us for a while up the coast, which they did. After a short week with us, they began their preparations for their long journey home, and we parted ways. To this day, I still think of Sylvie when I get around to making pizza, and I wonder where she is. We sadly lost all contact with them, but I wish I could tell her how grateful I still am that she forever enriched my culinary skills.

When we first left France, we had $20,000 in savings. We had whittled down a sizable chunk of that amount over our time in South America, so we decided it was time to start planning to find some new work. Our new target became Cayenne, French Guiana, just over the northern border from Brazil. The word on the water in French sailing circles was that work was easy to find in Cayenne for French expats since it was a French territory. So we set off, moseying along the Brazilian coast.

We soon came across Buzios, the islands of Abrolhos, and Bahia da Salvador—all tropical enclaves with their own particular flavors. In 1984, Buzios was touted as the quaint, new, South American version of St. Tropez. At the time, St. Tropez, on the French Riviera, was the European jet-setting vacation hotspot—the place for the rich and famous to see and be seen. We only planned to spend a day or two, but multiple chance encounters with several multinational expatriates led to unending invitations for breakfast, lunch, dinner, and cocktails. Ten days later, we finally extricated ourselves and moved on to Abrolhos, a collection of five little islands rising from coral reef outcroppings.

Designated a marine preserve and home to a small military outpost and lighthouse, Abrolhos provided a welcomed, isolated respite in nature. All four of us delighted in seeing the nesting birds and wild goats, as well as the slower change of pace. We had actually spotted Abrolhos over a year earlier on the horizon—it was the first land we spotted as we came nearer to the Brazilian coast. We stayed a day or two poking around the islands before continuing on.

From day one, when we first began our adventure with *Cowabunga,* our engine was an ongoing source of anxiety due to regular breakdowns. These difficulties often defined our trip and caused many unplanned and prolonged stops. We worried about the cost of repairs, searched for parts, waited on ordered parts, and even tried to manufacture parts at times. But many of these unpleasant engine-related experiences turned into memorable moments, sometimes fostering fond memories and friends for life despite the circumstances. Such was the case in Salvador da Bahia, or simply Bahia.

We anchored in the bay intending to have just a quick "look-see" visit to get the lay of the land, catch up on our mail from General Delivery at the American consulate, attend to some routine engine maintenance, and then continue on up the coast. After having accomplished the routine maintenance, Michel went to start up the engine and...nothing. He tried and tried, to no avail.

Over the next few days, Michel went down the diagnostic list of how to discern the problem. Nothing worked, so he reached out to some of the other boats in the anchorage. One person knew about this, and someone else knew about that. Someone had a certain tool, and someone else had another. Another fellow cruiser had the same engine and knew it backwards and forwards, he said. Slowly, our engine problem became the whole anchorage's problem. For almost three weeks, our engine was the focal point of most of the afternoon activity. A crowd amassed onboard *Cowabunga* each day with favorite wrenches, screwdrivers, and other what-nots for the latest round diagnostic session of the *Cowabunga* "repair-a-thon."

Since the engine was centrally located inside *Cowabunga*, the whole interior got progressively more crowded and cluttered while the engine was slowly dismantled. It was extremely difficult for us to do anything other than sleep there, so the kids and I became itinerant in that families from other boats took us aboard, fed us, or would take the kids during the day. In the evenings, we were wined and dined from one boat to another, and many impromptu parties erupted. We organized occasional outside tours in town together, and a couple of the older teenage girls became faithful, wonderful babysitters.

The Franco-Swiss family of Alec, Nadette, and their two children, Jim and Gougou, were lifesavers. Their boat, *Jakaranda*, stood out amongst every other in the anchorage—the hull was decked out in a striking violet-pink hue, like its namesake flower. The family onboard proved to be just as colorful. Alec was tall and lanky at his six feet,

always sporting a long blonde ponytail down his back. He was reserved, and always immersed in meticulous analyses of some matter
or other, be it a technical boat issue or the latest family communica-
tions from Switzerland. An extreme perfectionist, he could spend
hours devoted to the minute details of an issue. Nadette, a nickname
for "Bernadette," seemed an unlikely partner for Alex with her short
frizzy bob, extreme gregariousness, and a perpetual cigarette dangling
from her lips.

They were both down-to-earth, devoted parents to Gougou and
Jim who were about the same age and similar dispositions as our two
boys. Their shy and reserved daughter, Gougou, (Alec and Nadette
were incapable of explaining how that nickname was derived from
"Tina"), and bubbly son Jim became fast friends with Sean and Brendan. We eventually found out through many conversations that they
belonged to a societal elite far beyond our financial reach. Their boat,
Jakaranda, was a custom-built, comfortable sailboat. We could fully
stand up inside with plenty of individual space. It was almost cavernous, and for a cruising monohull that was amazing!

Alec also had a dedicated, well-equipped workshop onboard. A lot
of our engine ended up there in various pieces. Also, since we couldn't
charge our batteries with the engine dismantled, *Jakaranda* lifted their
anchor and tied up alongside *Cowabunga* on occasion, running their engine to charge us up. Since all four kids got along well, our side-by-
side afternoon sessions proved to be a magical solution to keeping all
the children occupied and happy in each other's company, and we parents were soothed.

With all this communal help, the engine was eventually put back
into working order. We were overwhelmed by everyone's generosity
and decided to throw a thank-you party. After tallying up the number
of people who helped us out, we realized that *Cowabunga* was too small
to house a party for over twenty people, so again *Jakaranda* came to

our aid and rafted up alongside us. With two deck widths to spread out, we hosted a party to remember.

By now it was June, and again our time frame had been impacted. But despite this, we set out to explore a bit of the island of Itaparica in the bay, and also headed up the Paraguaçu River as we forayed to a secluded waterfall and the waterfront village of Maragogipe. A Saturday morning market was quaint and colorful with the local country folk and merchants, and cargo-laden burros crowding the plaza with wares for sale. Brazilian *saveiros*, local, flat-bottomed, barge-type sailing vessels, followed the tides. Loaded with varied loads of grains and odd goods, they painted an otherworldly tableau as they plied the waters of the Paraguaçu River and the greater Bahia area. We eventually set out for Fortaleza, which would be our northernmost and last Brazilian destination.

A few days out from Bahia and making good progress up the Brazilian coast under pleasant conditions, we were suddenly intrigued by the idea of making an unscheduled stop at St. Joao de Pessoa. After reading some brief nautical instructions and studying the charts, it seemed like a pleasant spot and a good opportunity to catch up on a night or two of uninterrupted sleep. The kids could stretch their legs a bit on land, too.

The chart showed a lot of reefs, shallow areas, and underwater rocks. But it was high tide, and Michel was confident after reading the nautical instructions that we could take a short cut, avoiding the longer, winding marked route. I preferred, however, that we follow a freighter just ahead of us that was entering via the channel. Michel insisted we could take the short cut over the reefs, and we began to argue vehemently about it. Just then, the wind whipped through and grabbed the chart in question from the cockpit table, whisking it away overboard. We were both cut short, our mouths agape having lost our only valid tool to enter the port. We both blamed each other, but our decision was made for us. There was no choice but to head back out to sea, to our original target on this leg of our journey.

A night or two before our arrival in Fortaleza, we were perplexed when we came upon little bobbing white lights, low and widespread on the water. They weren't normal navigation lights, and as we closed in on them, we saw they were simple, flickering kerosene lamps. The lights surrounded us, and we could make out what looked like planks, the length and width of windsurfing boards, but rough-hewn wooden versions. They had primitive wooden masts, furled cloth sails, a bench, a box, and a few other sundry articles scattered about onboard. In the dark and fleeting lamp light, we couldn't see any people on these vessels.

Later we learned that the local primitive skiffs were called a *jangadas*, and typically five to eight fishermen would set out to sea on one of these for a week of fishing! There were no sideboards or any construction that would prevent water from spilling over. For sleeping at night, they lie down, side by side like sardines, surrounded by big sponges to stop some of the water from sloshing over them. Typically, they would venture a hundred miles or so from the coast. We marveled at how they made their way back to home port without any navigation device whatsoever.

A desolate place in a years-long drought, Fortaleza was every bit a desert with a dune-like landscape. It wasn't uncommon to see hunger-stricken children with distended stomachs wandering naked in town. Nevertheless, the city of Fortaleza was trying to capitalize on its potential for tourism, with its unrelenting sun and wide beaches. Some new flashy high-rise apartments, condos, and hotels flanked the waterfront, and the city sponsored a lively open-air bazaar in the evenings, trying to lure visitors to the cafés with a festive atmosphere. Unfortunately, so much widespread poverty mingling with tourists was a perfect recipe for jealousy and robbery.

CHAPTER SIXTEEN

Fortaleza, Brazil

There weren't many sailboats present upon our arrival in the anchorage. We got the lowdown from one family that another boat recently had a scary experience, having been boarded and robbed. One had to be vigilant here. Consequently, we decided to never leave the boat alone or go into town all together. This reinforced our intention to stay briefly in Fortaleza—just enough time to fill up on some provisions, rest a day or two, and head on to French Guiana.

That night, I heard a thud. I was always the first one to hear a noise or feel the change in the sway of the boat at anchor. I'm not good at sensing from what direction the wind is coming, but I do know when something is amiss. It took a few seconds for me to fully awaken and realize that I had heard a noise. Then something told me to hoist myself up through the hatch to take a quick, reassuring look. I hoped to prove to myself that I really didn't hear anything but came face to face with a mustachioed young man on our deck. I scared him; he scared me. I tried to scream, but nothing came out. I absolutely froze. He swiftly jumped into his little wooden dinghy, cut the line, and drifted out into the darkness. Then with horror, I suddenly saw an item of our navigation equipment lying on the deck with the wires cut. He hadn't just been arriving, he had already been down below with a knife while we were sleeping.

Somehow I remembered to awaken Michel (who was still asleep!). While he groped for his glasses, I scrambled up front to the kids' cabin to check on them; they were fine and asleep. I noticed Michel's wallet on the chart table and remembered there had been a $100 in there from an exchange he had done earlier that day. I just assumed the money was gone. All the while I was shouting to Michel a rapid-fire reconstruction what must have happened.

"The kids are OK, but he has a knife, he cut the equipment connections, took the money, our foul weather gear is missing..."

Michel had grabbed the rifle he kept at the ready near our bed. I didn't like having a weapon onboard, and Michel wasn't terribly keen on it either. Possessing or using guns was never a part of our lifestyle, but we felt obligated to purchase one before leaving on our trip. Piracy was a real threat in certain waters, and although not a likely possibility where we would be sailing, it could occur. With the drug-running trade at the time, we knew of a few hijacked sailboats showing up in Miami without the rightful owners.

I joined Michel on deck, and we could still see the intruder off in the distance. Michel shouted for him to stop and fired two warning shots. The thief dove from his tiny boat into the water, letting his little dinghy go adrift.

We lowered our own dinghy down into the water and then, like a posse after our outlaw, the two of us took off across the water. I handled the outboard and Michel literally rode shotgun. We were determined to get our gear back, although it probably wasn't the smartest thing to do.

There were a lot of fishing trawlers where we saw the intruder jump into the water. We weaved in and out among the boats, looking for a swimmer. With only some intermittent light from the onshore port lights, it was too dark to see much of anything, and we never found him. We retrieved his dinghy and were able to take back some of our clothes that were still on it, and even some of his. However, our foul weather gear must have blown off and was lost. Then we purposely let his boat go, giving him the rawest end of the deal that we could.

We returned to *Cowabunga* and tried to regain our composure. Despite our efforts to keep our guard up, we still couldn't believe that someone would brazenly come on board in the middle of the night while we were sleeping. All our navigation equipment was still there. The item on the deck was apparently his first attempt to take some of the equipment, after having first loaded the other items. Then we noticed that Michel's wallet still had the $100. He either missed it, or I foiled his chance.

The next morning, Michel reported our encounter to the police. Their attitude was fairly nonchalant, and they even chided Michel for having "missed his mark" when he fired the warning shots! "Too bad you missed him," they said. "It would have been one less problem for us to deal with." After that, we were good and ready to leave Fortaleza as soon as possible.

The morning after our jarring midnight encounter with the intruder, Michel and I were sitting outside in the cockpit, drinking our coffee and rehashing what had happened, when a small motorboat came alongside *Cowabunga*. Miguel Maccio, an Argentinian, was from Columbia University's Lamont-Doherty Geological Observatory in New York. He said he urgently needed passage to St. Peter and St. Paul Rocks for a scientific mission for the university. Still shaken, we were wary as Miguel approached, wondering what this might have to do with the previous night. The more he elaborated, however, we could see that he was earnest in his mission. Miguel explained that the

Lamont-Doherty Geological Observatory maintained a wind recording station on the Rocks, but something was malfunctioning and he
needed to get out there quickly.

Routinely, a team from the observatory visited the site via a French
oceanography ship. But for this sudden, last minute trip, the ship was
not available. Having arrived just two days earlier in Fortaleza, Miguel
had a prior agreement with a local fishing vessel crew to take him out
to St. Peter and St. Paul. But he quickly canceled the deal once he saw
the appalling condition of their boat, and realized they had no idea how
to chart a course to St. Peter and St. Paul Rocks. He said he had been
intrigued by the American flag flying from our stern. Miguel figured
that if we had gotten this far under our own steam, we must know
what we're doing. He sweetened his request with the offer of a $5,000
contract. We were very tempted.

But it was a tall order. St. Peter and St. Paul Rocks are very tiny,
rocky outcroppings made up of fifteen small islets (some of which really are only rocks) that lie about halfway between Africa and South
America. Although technically in the North Atlantic, for all intents and
purposes, they practically sit on the equator at just slightly over 60
miles north of the line. A Brazilian territory, St. Peter and St. Paul
Rocks are the exposed jagged tips of the pinnacles of an underwater
mountain ridge known as an "abyssal mantle." This area came under
scrutiny and international infamy for the part it played in the crash of
Air France Flight 447, from Rio de Janeiro to Paris, May 31, 2009.
Some of the aircraft fragments were found near St. Peter and St. Paul
Rocks.

Aside from the money windfall, it was also a unique opportunity
to discover a practically unknown place and to gain a feather in our cap
to have run a mission for Columbia University. Nevertheless, we were
still skeptical to take this on. Miguel had quite a bit of equipment he
would have to load on board, along with several crates, and five large

storage batteries. After much discussion and thought, we decided that the kids and I would stay in a little hotel near the beach while Michel, Miguel, and another crewmate that Miguel hired would make the trip. It just didn't seem fair to make the kids endure what would surely be very unpleasant sailing conditions for at least a week, nor oblige Miguel to be cooped up with two small (most likely cranky) children.

It took a week to prepare. Along with provisioning *Cowabunga* with food, fuel, and finding spots for Miguel's equipment, the paperwork for the Brazilian authorities was a whole other undertaking. The trip was a fiasco from the get-go, and when they just left Fortaleza, barely a day into the voyage, they were met with beating headwinds. The forestay turnbuckle (a vital tension-adjusting device) broke. This was a major misfortune in that the full genoa sail, normally hoisted at the head of the boat, could not be used. Without the turnbuckle, the genoa sail force would be too much of a load on the rigging, especially in the strong 25-30 knot headwinds. Michel was able to craft a temporary replacement, but it was still wise to use a smaller headsail instead. This meant sailing at a much slower speed, and much more difficulty in battling the counter-current.

Compounding this bad luck, the diesel fuel tank sprang a leak shortly thereafter, not only sloshing diesel fuel throughout the bilge but also up along the insides of the hull, behind the water tanks, bookshelves, provision cupboards, behind the galley, fridge...everywhere. There is nothing worse than smelly, greasy diesel fuel permeating the air and coating everything while being confined within a sealed cocoon. The hatches couldn't even be opened for fresh air since the winds caused the choppy sea to constantly slosh over the deck.

Making things even worse, the hired-on Brazilian crewmember began to panic. He was incapable of handling the mishaps and uncomfortable sailing conditions, and his mental state rendered living conditions for all others on board intolerable. Thus, Michel and Miguel decided to turn back, returning several days later to Fortaleza. The obnoxious crewmember couldn't get on land fast enough. He was neither heard from nor seen again.

While I was on land in the hotel, the kids and I were able to keep in constant contact with Michel through the ham radio and a network of amateur radio buffs on land that would call me in our hotel room. We welcomed their safe return. Consulting with Miguel, the three of us reassessed the situation. Miguel wasn't ready to give up; he wanted to try again once repairs were made, but this time with the kids and me as crew. He was willing to bet that we would be more competent and easier to get along with than the prior failed crewmate.

Brazil being Brazil at the time, importing and buying new foreign-made parts to accomplish the necessary repairs was prohibitively expensive. I was able to find a replacement turnbuckle from a fellow cruiser's spare parts, and local laborers were often skilled at creating or copying parts satisfactorily. We had a new, custom, stainless-steel diesel fuel tank made up in no time. However, it was a big job cutting out the old tank first, then cleaning up the fuel mess inside the boat before installing the new one. After a very hectic week, they set sail again, but this time with the kids and me.

We had ten days of sailing against the trade winds, making very little progress on a daily basis to cover the 600-mile trip. Much like our experience of sailing out of Buenos Aires on the Rio de la Plata, it was very hot and humid. No air could circulate inside the boat since we had to keep all the hatches closed tight. Water from the choppy sea constantly sloshed over the deck, and once seawater splashes inside a boat, it never dries out. Cooking was not an easy chore since the conditions were so choppy, and the stove only intensified the cabin heat. It felt like we were living in a pressure cooker.

In spite of such unpleasant living conditions, Miguel was a pleasure to have onboard. He fit right in with our family routine and proved to be a saint. With two small boys of his own, he was very patient and helped with the kids, the chores, and the cooking. It wasn't easy for Sean and Brendan, either. They couldn't go out on the deck since conditions were so rough, and their cabin space was significantly impacted with Miguel's crates and equipment. But by occupying themselves with their toys and playing games with each other, interspersed with meals, nap times, and story hours with Miguel and us, they managed.

Halfway through the trip, discouragement increased. We had reached the same latitude as St. Peter and St. Paul Rocks but were stopped dead in the water. Michel's sextant sun sights kept giving us the same position for two straight days, and it seemed we weren't making any easterly headway toward our destination. We just couldn't beat the forces from the trade winds and the head-on counter current. Miguel even began to harbor doubts about Michel's navigating abilities. So, on the advice of Captain Michel, we charted a new course due north, a significant distance out of our way, gambling that at an appropriate angle, the current and the winds would assist us in a southerly heading, dead on to our destination.

On day ten, shortly after dawn, Michel announced: "My calculations say we are here; I keep getting the same position. We have arrived." Yet, from the deck, we saw nothing. None of us saw anything. No land. "It has to be there," he affirmed after taking another sun sight with the sextant. He had been taking sun sights almost non-stop since daybreak. A lot was at stake. We were trying to find a needle in a haystack, or just about, it seemed. Finally, Michel climbed the mast and confirmed the sextant's headings. The "there" was there! He spied the Rocks in the hazy distance, and we were relieved and elated. His gamble paid off.

In the grand scheme of the vastness of the Atlantic Ocean, this archipelago is extremely tiny. Its highest point only measures only about sixty feet above sea level. Only five miles away, St. Peter and St. Paul Rocks barely poked above the haze. Most any other landfall would have risen considerably above sea level, easily visible from twenty miles or so. We were all relieved to see it given Michel's reputation as a navigator was at stake, and also the fulfillment of our mission.

Within a couple of hours, the bow of *Cowabunga* headed into the tight, horseshoe-shaped bay of the Rocks. Partially protected by two rocky, pinnacle guardians that faced each other across the narrow entrance, the incoming waves were slightly quelled as they broke on these two sentries. Even though these natural jetties subdued the waves, the swell still rushed into the bay, sloshing water from one rocky side to the other like a swimming pool full of jumping kids. We were able to indicate that the bay should be about 40-50 feet deep and feasible for anchoring. However, our depth sounder consistently indicated otherwise—over 655 feet deep. Michel and Miguel decided to try and set the anchor anyway—several times in several spots. They repeatedly let out our 195 feet of chain, only to reel it all in again and again. It was useless.

Now what? There was no beach, no dock, no platform for tying up. Besides, even if it was shallow enough, there still wasn't enough swing room to allow for a safe anchorage without crashing against the rocks. We didn't sail all this distance under such difficult conditions just to turn around and go back. It was time for some creative thinking, and Michel excelled at that.

The trade winds and the current were constant this time of year, we could depend upon that. Banking on nature's cooperation, Michel and Miguel set up two long mooring lines from each side of the bow of our boat, tying up to each of the "guardian pinnacle" rocks at the bay's entrance. With the dinghy, they motored out and lassoed each rock, tethering *Cowabunga* securely. The constant, regular wind was helpful, keeping us at bay and out of danger from banging into the rocks. Even though we had arrived in the early morning, it was an all-day effort to settle things. We were finally able to relax by sunset, savoring a well-deserved evening meal while surveying the surreal, eerie scene before us.

Perched on the equator at the mouth of the bay, we felt like we had a view from on top of the world. We all agreed that it must be the closest landscape on Earth to resemble what we imagined the Moon would look like. Not a speck of green—no vegetation whatsoever. It was a volcanic landscape of coarse, dark lava pinnacles and strangely coiffed crags snowcapped with guano. The Rocks teemed with bird life, while the bay was said to be chock-full of sharks. We could see the bird life everywhere, and we hoped that the sharks weren't as numerous as rumors held, but we maintained a safe distance anyway—no swimming in this bay.

After a restful night, Michel and Miguel set to work. Getting on the Rocks was not a piece of cake. There was no beach or flat surface to land the dinghy. It was all rocky cliffs, with only one viable spot sporting two natural "footholds." These were moving targets under the constant, heaving swell that crashed against the rocks. Miguel and Michel had to balance themselves on these footholds while placing equipment on the flat surface just above the cliff's edge, just barely an arm's length away. They spent most of the first day making trips back and forth between *Cowabunga* and the cliff footholds, loading and unloading equipment in a delicate dance of "balance-heave-ho," all while gauging the swells. Miguel was finally able to set up a working base at the foot of the wind recording station and began the process of determining what the problem could be.

The station itself wasn't very elaborate, but given that this was 1984, it embodied the most sophisticated computer and satellite technology for the time. A wind vane atop a pole relayed information to a computer, which communicated that information to a satellite twice a day. This data was then relayed from the satellite to the Lamont-Doherty Geological Laboratory at Columbia University in New York for various meteorological studies they were conducting. Every evening we would call a ham radio contact person for a pre-arranged appointment. He would "phone-patch" us into the Lamont-Doherty laboratory whereupon Miguel and his colleagues would collaborate to decipher the information that had or had not been transmitted that day. This process went on for about five days, and Michel assisted Miguel when and wherever he could.

The kids and I were anxious to go on land and explore this savage and intriguing environment, especially after having been confined to the boat for the ten-day sail. As it happened, our second day there was my thirtieth birthday, and we all decided to celebrate it on land with a unique barbecue. Among the hearty bounty of bird and fish life, legend also held that lobsters were quite plentiful due to the rocky environment devoid of fishermen. We had brought along a lobster trap just in case, which Michel had already prepared and set in the water the day before.

Attempting a landing with the dinghy—especially with our two small boys—involved careful, tricky footwork. But Michel and Miguel were old hands at the procedure by now. Once we managed to heave the boys and ourselves over the rocky ledge, it was breathtaking. A rocky plateau spread out before us, dotted with innumerable tidal pools. It bristled with a gleaming carpet of peculiar, one-armed crabs, which ran around and around, waving their single menacing claws (which were really quite cute). Flying fish that had flown too high dotted the rocks. Spectacular, noisy waves crashed over the cliffs, rocks, and pinnacles, and our view of the landscape from the boat was confirmed: there was no vegetation whatsoever.

True to their reputation, the bird population was large and aggressive. They attempted to overpower and threaten us, having no fear of humans since they rarely had contact. They would rush, dive-bomb, and cackle at us, especially those with a few young ones in their nests. After a while, we all seemed to reach a truce, and a certain invisible boundary was established. One step beyond that frontier, though, and they launched into attack mode.

The unbelievable surprise and joy of the day was our lobster catch of thirty lobsters for my thirtieth birthday! It was amazing. In the hopes that we might catch a few lobsters, we brought a barbecue grill and some wood scraps with us. Michel was able to stoke up a respectable fire and our afternoon lobster grill was a success. Not only did we feast on them right then and there, but I also had my job cut out cooking and preserving as much as I could for future meals since there was so much.

It was fun to watch Sean and Brendan be so inspired by these surroundings. They were, of course, used to water, isolated beaches, tropical anchorages, and unique natural settings. But this was different for them, and they were enthralled while poking around the tidal pools and learning to respect these birds and crabs that weren't afraid of them. We were even able to explore the twisted and rusted iron remnants of an old abandoned lighthouse. There were commemorative plaques left from the few ships that had passed this way over the years. We added one for *Cowabunga* to this unique and privileged collection.

Back on deck, we continually saw large, dark figures darting underwater, confirming the presence of sharks in the bay. One moonless evening after dinner, inspired by a bit of mischievousness, Michel decided to shine a powerful light onto the surface of the water. The effect incited a flurry of flying fish to jump out of the water, landing all over the deck. At 10-12 inches long, they were the largest flying fish we had ever seen. This set into motion a chain reaction as the sharks became crazed and rallied after the flying fish. The water churned with their blind fury, and they rammed against the hull of the boat, creating showers of fish that rained down.

Michel and Miguel took it one step further, deciding to play "chicken" and taunted these underwater phantoms. Loading an industrial-grade fishing line with a heavy-duty gauge hook and flying fish as bait, they secured the line to a winch and large deck cleat. It didn't take long for the first shark to strike the bait. Michel and Miguel started to slowly reel it in with the winch, and just as it was about to come alongside the boat, the shark effortlessly broke the line with a sudden jerk. They repeated their "fishing" several times, and each time the sharks snapped the line. Although merely an evening's entertainment, it was a vivid reminder of the power nature wielded in this isolated spot of the world.

Sean was five years old at this time and had developed a passion for fishing. We had a cast net on board that he had become adept at handling, throwing it handily in the water from our deck when we were at anchor. With the abundant schools of fish pooling around the boat, Sean was anxious to catch some, and he found that by simply throwing cracker crumbs overboard, the fish crowded around to gobble them up. Then he just threw the net on top of the churning group below, catching plenty of fish to fulfill our daily needs.

The wind and swells intensified during our time there, and one afternoon the dinghy broke loose from *Cowabunga*, drifting to the other side of the bay. There was no choice but for Michel to jump into the water and swim over to retrieve it. Mindful of all the sharks down below, he was extremely nervous and swam with all the speed he could muster, splashing frantically with each stroke until he finished the heart-pounding swim. We were all relieved when he managed to reach it quickly without incident.

The next day, as the wind and swells continued to grow, both "umbilical" ropes that tethered the boat to the bay's entrance kept inching up higher and higher toward the top of the rocks. In particular, the port line crept up to a dangerous point where we feared it would no longer be securely attached, and possibly even heave right off with the next big wave. Michel and Miguel rowed over in the dinghy to try and push it back down. Michel carefully gauged the swells so he could jump onto the rock, steady himself, and deal with the line. He succeeded and was juggling the job while waves crashed around him, when suddenly, one huge wave blasted down on top of the pinnacle, throwing Michel to the water where he was gobbled up by the white froth below. Miguel panicked in the dinghy as he searched the water around him. The boys and I watched from the deck, and we couldn't believe that he disappeared before eyes. My heart stopped; Sean screamed desperately, "Mon Papa, mon Papa!" Then after briefly pondering the situation, Sean said, "Oh, that's OK. If we have no more Papa, Miguel can be our Papa now." Although I was frantic at the moment, I tried to reassure him that Papa was still there and would be okay.

It seemed forever before Michel popped out of the angry foam. His glasses were gone, and he was bruised and cut up from having been mashed against the rocks. Later he confided that he was sure that was the end for him. Much later, we were able to laugh about Sean's solution for a new papa. He and Miguel did manage to set the line properly on a second try. It was a sobering experience, and we vowed from that moment on that any further visits to the Rocks would require wearing lifejackets—a stupid oversight.

We stayed a total of five days, finally leaving with haste as the anchoring situation seemed to become more precarious every day. I didn't dare let the boys out on deck anymore. The boat rocked violently, and I couldn't risk either one of them losing their balance with the waiting sharks below. Miguel decided that he accomplished as much as he could with the station. Although thrilled to have experienced this unique spot, we anxiously threw off the ties that bound us and made a speedy, five-day sail back to Fortaleza. After the ten-day slog uphill to get to St. Peter and St. Paul Rocks, the return trip was a breeze.

We had grown accustomed to having Miguel on board; he fit in well with our routine. But with the mission accomplished, we sadly bid him goodbye. Miguel returned to New York, and soon after we left Brazil in our wake. It was bittersweet. Brazil had been our home and base for a year and a half. We felt like we knew and understood Brazil. But we also anticipated new adventures, and with our added cushion of $5,000, we could travel longer than we had anticipated.

Back at sea, our compass heading now targeted Cayenne, French Guiana where we still intended to look for work and settle in for a few months. Hopefully, it would also be a good place for Sean to start kindergarten in September.

Just beginning to live on Cowabunga, a weekend outing near Bordeaux, me with Sean, one year old.

Janis, Sean, and Brendan in the early days of life on board, in the port of Le Verdon, spring 1982.

Summer 1982, with Brendan, about four months old, in our home port of Le Verdon, France.

Last picture taken of us by our fisherman friend, Michou, leaving Le Verdon, France, as we head out to cross the Bay of Biscay for La Coruña, Spain. August 29, 1982.

*In the Lagoon at Dakar, Sean and Brendan playing in our "baby-proofed"
netted area that we set around the mast on deck, December 1982.*

Sean saluting our friendly escorts.

Cowabunga, anchored at the foot of the Pão de Açúcar, or Sugarloaf Mountain, in Rio de Janeiro's Guanabara Bay.

Michel showing Sean and Brendan the finer points of navigating at the chart table.

Brendan, eighteen months, proudly and deftly guiding the tiller.
Sean, three years old.

Michel, Janis, Sean, and Brendan (in the backpack) in Buenos Aires' Plaza de
Mayo for the inauguration of Raoul Alfonsin, December 10, 1983.

Brendan and Sean in a stand-off with resident birds on St. Peter and St. Paul rocks, off the coast of Brazil, July 1984.

An abandoned prison cell block on Ile St. Joseph, adjacent to Devil's Island, part of the Iles du Salut group off the coast of French Guiana, April 1985.

Cowabunga in a calm sea at dusk.

The iconic dragon of Dragon Point, tip of Merritt Island, in Indian Harbour Beach on the Intracoastal Waterway, Florida.

The Shack, on the tip of Merritt Island, that was our home base for three years from 1985 to 1988.

Brendan, Janis, Michel, and Sean on the Shack's dock, with Cowabunga anchored in the background.

Michel, Janis, Brendan, and Sean anchored in the Intracoastal Waterway, Indian Harbour Beach, 1985-1988.

Sean, about six or seven years old, learning how to sail solo with our homemade rigged dinghy in Florida.

Brendan, Michel, and Sean during our hike in Nueva Gerona, on the Isla de Juventud, Cuba.

Brendan, six years old, relaxing on a calm day at sea.

Our cozy camping spot in the Sierra Maestra mountains, above El Portillo, Cuba, January 1989.

Some of the kids of Spanish Water, Curaçao, with Brendan, seven years old, and Sean, ten years old, in the foreground.

*Above: Cuna woman and
her children in the San
Blas Islands, coming for
a chat and some mola
trading.*

*Right: Sean and
Brendan's cabin, the V-
berth, in the front of the
boat. They shared their
space with the sails, their
schoolbooks, and Legos.
Each item had its assigned
place.*

Above: Sean and Brendan in the foreground, with another family, on a San Blas beach, October 1989.

Left: Sean's prize Dorado catch that he caught with his homemade kitchen spoon lure.

Left: Sean (ten years old) and Brendan (seven years old) in their cabin.

Below: Cowabunga tied up to the dock at one of the typical casas de pescas that we encountered along the Cuban coast.

Above: Michel puts on some final touches for Cowabunga's final cleaning haul out in Bodega Bay, California, shortly after our arrival.

Right: Cowabunga all cleaned up at her final destination in Bodega Bay, California, July 1990.

Cowabunga looking her finest at anchor. A wind generator hanging in the rigging in the front of the boat supplied power for the batteries for lights and equipment on board. A barbecue and the self-steering wind vane are at the back of the boat.

The Cowabunga Crew all grown up in 2014. Left to right, Sean, Michel, Brendan, Janis.

CHAPTER SEVENTEEN

CAYENNE, FRENCH GUIANA

It was a hot, hazy dawn, and we were gliding along 100 miles or so off the northern coast of South America. It had been a restful and peaceful sail so far: no accidents, no broken equipment, no strange noises emanating from the bowels of the boat. According to the charts, we were in oil platform territory, so Michel had traced our course to avoid them. Up until now, we hadn't seen any, and we were particularly vigilant on our night watches even though Michel thought our route put us well north of that area. Then, off on the horizon, I saw a platform.

I turned the watch duty over to Michel, and while he settled in the cockpit, I went down below to get some coffee. We were sailing at a comfortable angle, and the wind was accommodating, just right for brewing the morning coffee without having to brace myself tightly in the galley corner. I went to see to the kids and get breakfast going before taking my well-deserved nap. Michel kept me apprised of the ever-approaching platform. It seemed we were getting closer and most likely would have to change our course. Then, he saw the anchor lines and a helicopter landing pad. I quickly finished what I was doing so I could head back up on deck to help with necessary maneuvers and sail changes for our course.

I popped into the cockpit and peered out to the front of the boat and saw...nothing. Only blue water surrounded us for 360° as far as I could see.

"Where did it go?" I asked Michel.

"That's what I'm wondering," he marveled.

It was bizarre. We both saw it, and then we both didn't see it. Was it a ghostly figure? How could we both imagine the same thing and it not be real? Dumbfounded for several minutes, we both began to think it may have been a mirage. Neither Michel nor I had ever seen such a thing and we certainly never imagined a mirage to be such a solid, tangible image with precise details. We questioned each other.

I grabbed a dictionary that explained it perfectly: "a phenomenon occurring under certain atmospheric conditions in a desert or at sea, and often in equatorial latitudes; an optical illusion of an actual object situated several miles away and refracted to appear in another location."[2] Our location and current weather conditions seem to fit this scenario perfectly. There were real oil platforms in the area (albeit at least 100 miles away), and we were near the equator. Apparently, the early morning haze and the sun created the ideal conditions to reflect the image elsewhere.

We arrived in Cayenne, French Guiana a day or two after our mirage sighting, and we were undeniably in Amazonian territory. The predominance of this mighty river was all around us: dense jungle foliage and coffee-with-cream-colored water. As far away as we were from the mouth of the Amazon, that mighty river still tainted the deep

[2] See also "Fata Morgana" or "Sea Mirage"

blue ocean a muddy hue. Surprisingly, in that same vicinity, the ocean even tasted fresh!

French Guiana sits just above the equator around the latitude of 4° north. An unlikely settlement on the fringes of the jungle, Cayenne seemed to barely keep the wilds of the jungle at bay, with the dense green and humid tropical forest gobbling up the main road just a mile or two outside the city limits. Anchored in the Cayenne River estuary, we were surrounded by the same thick, milk chocolate-colored waters as the Amazon and its tributaries. The red chili, or Cayenne pepper, originates from Cayenne and is aptly named after this city. The equatorial heat and diverse people added a touch of spice that never ceased to surprise us. Although it's not a tropical paradise, we found it to be a tropical treasure.

Everything grew bigger here. Super-sized, two-inch long "palmetto" cockroaches occasionally landed on our deck. Once, a fist-sized beetle dive-bombed through the main hatch, right into my galley sink as I was washing the dishes! While walking on the harbor wharf, I almost blindly stepped on a prehistoric-looking, jumbo-sized insect, and during a family camping expedition deep in the jungle, giant oversized centipedes known as *scolopends* crawled amidst some of the overhead rafters. Those creepy crawlers can grow up to twelve inches long and are actually quite poisonous.

On other occasions while on inland excursions, we were hypnotized by flashes of deep luminescent blue, as morpho butterflies flew past us with their five-to-eight-inch wingspans. Some intrepid souls we met from other boats indulged their fancy for evening sightings of caimans, which are a reptile related to alligators and crocodiles. By venturing out at night, the sightseers would target the reptile's telltale red eyes poised on a river surface with flashlights, and follow the caimans as they glided just below the waterline.

The reality of being in Amazon forest territory really hit us a few weeks later while we were on a family sightseeing trip. We were forced to stop our loaner car in the middle of the road for a long spell—the time it took for a sloth to cross the road (a really long time!). It seemed like something out of a cartoon, with every movement carefully articulated in slow motion.

"C'est quoi, c'est quoi? What is it?" the boys asked.

"Will you look at that—a *paresseux*!" Michel noted. I think that was the first time I learned the name of the animal in French. We were all amazed and got out of the car to get a better look. The sloth may have been afraid of us, but by its very nature, it didn't scurry off.

French Guiana is a *département* of France (comparable in status as one of the U.S.'s states), having evolved from its former existence as a French colony. Seeking work here was perfectly legal for us since Michel is French and I had full legal French resident status. In short order, Michel found work in an architect's office, and I found a part time job as a bilingual secretary with an American shrimping company. Sean soon started kindergarten, and Brendan accompanied me to work, where I was able to leave him with a babysitter (one of the fishermen's wives). He spent the mornings with Desirée and her little girl, Tasha, in their simple cottage on the shrimping compound grounds, just a few doors from my office.

Our seven-month sojourn in this jungle way station was far from boring. The anchorage was filled with approximately fifty boats, mostly French cruising families, all in temporary "civilian" modes: jobs, children in school, or some sort of reevaluation of their travels and sailing life. Rush hour occurred every weekday at 8 a.m. when a wave of dinghies carried families, couples, and the occasional solo sailor to a landlubber's 9 a.m. to 5 p.m. routine. It was one such morning that I had the scare of my life.

"Aren't you afraid they'll fall overboard? Don't you keep them attached?" our non-boating friends would ask about Sean and Brendan. The thought scared me, and I often considered the what-ifs. But kids also get hit by cars simply running out into the street in front of their homes, and drown in swimming pools in their backyards. Our daily reality was that it was not feasible to have our children bound up in lifejackets twenty-four hours a day. We had childproofed the boat as much as possible and were constantly vigilant as to their whereabouts. I couldn't constantly worry about "what-if."

One particular morning, Brendan and I left for the shore with a friend in her dinghy. Converging at the dock with a half-dozen others bound for work and school, she turned off the outboard as we came alongside the dock and prepared to tie-up. The dock was above me at eye level, and the current was running strong in the opaque water. I picked Brendan up, raising him above my head to set him on the dock. I couldn't see the boards on the dock, so when I set Brendan down, I had no idea that I set him directly above a hole. It was just his size, and he slid right through down into the muck and was gone.

He disappeared from sight, and I was absolutely petrified. My heart raced, and I searched for him in every direction—I looked for any part of him, any sign of him, anywhere. Then I frantically reached into the water and splashed about, trying to catch him.

There were quite a few of us coming to the dock, and everyone saw it happen, panicking in turn. My friend who brought us ashore, and who was very pregnant, instinctively jumped in after Brendan since she was downstream from where he fell, thinking she could catch him, but she couldn't find him either. The minutes or seconds that passed seemed an agonizing eternity.

Then suddenly, Brendan's arm popped up out of the water, and someone in a nearby dinghy grabbed it. He was shaken, white with shock, and had drunk quite a bit of water. It took us a while to calm down, get our wits about us, and get Brendan cleaned up. Since he was only two, I don't think he remembers it as vividly as I do, or probably not at all. For me, it was much more traumatic than his previous plunge in Florianopolis six months earlier, and it still haunts me today.

Although we were lucky, that wasn't the case for a fellow cruising family with us in Cayenne. Many months later we learned of the drowning of little three-year-old Alice aboard *Myositis*, shortly after our departure. Her parents were on board, along with several other people and their children, as well. She just slipped out of sight, long enough for it to be too late. It was even more heartbreaking in that both her parents were doctors, and were unable save their child despite their desperate efforts. Contrary to what non-sailors may think, such stories are few and far between. Yet they serve as reminders that in this chosen lifestyle, we must always remain vigilant.

By this time in his short life of five years, Sean had already attended pre-school in France and Brazil. This would be his first real classroom experience, and a first being in the minority being a white child. The native Creole population of French Guiana is black, and there were very few white children in the school. It was a curious turnaround for us, and on occasion, we experienced prejudice and racism towards the white population.

It was also a first for Brendan to spend a few hours away from us and in a daycare situation. Brendan was reserved and timid, and not particularly outgoing at this stage in his life. It was a bit wrenching for both of us when I first began to leave him in the mornings, the event punctuated by his frantic sobs. Desirée, his nanny, assured me that it didn't last long and he eventually warmed up to her and her daughter. It was hard to willfully put him through such distress, but I knew I couldn't always spare him certain sorrows; it was part of growing up.

The anchorage in Cayenne became a real community. Upon our return to the dock in the evenings, many of us would linger, socialize, do a bit of laundry in the bathroom sink on the wharf, or set up impromptu dinner invitations. A rustic shower had also been installed for our use by the city on the wharf, and it was a welcomed convenience. One couple also indulged their entrepreneurial spirit and invested in a food truck where we would gather for a beer and some good cheer while the kids scampered about. Amongst the many families in the anchorage, we counted around thirty children in the mix. We had made friends earlier with many of these cruising families at various stops in Brazil, and it was nice for all the kids to have the opportunity to spend several months together. Christmas was just around the corner, and many of the adults decided it would be fun to mark the occasion for the kids.

There was an old Brazilian *tapouille* boat in the anchorage—a flat-bottomed, barge-like sailing vessel used on the Amazon and surrounding rivers to ship goods from place to place. It was in decent shape, big with a nice interior space, and it sat idle in the anchorage. The owner agreed to let all us cruisers use it for a Christmas party. What started out as something humble turned into a huge extravaganza as participation grew. We collected money to buy a present for each child and cornered a volunteer to play Santa. A talented seamstress among us was able to create a very respectable Santa costume out of a red, king-size bed sheet that I donated to the cause.

The day of the party, everyone brought food, and Santa ceremoniously entered the cavernous space below the tapouille's deck, before sitting regally amongst the children. Each child approached Santa for a gift. It was the first time Brendan had seen Santa, and he was hesitant. Sean couldn't believe his good fortune. Santa in the flesh! In true French fashion, the potluck event was overflowing with gourmet items, and we all felt blessed with genuine Christmas cheer. Over fifty people partied into the night.

The actual town of Cayenne was pleasant and had colorful, Caribbean colonial architecture from the 1800s. Nestled right up to the harbor, the town was easy to get around on foot or bicycle. The population was a spicy cocktail of native Creoles, mainland French expats, Brazilians, Haitians, Surinamese, British Guyanans of Indian descent, Hmong refugees from Laos (who mainly lived in Cacao, a settlement ensconced in the jungle), Lebanese, and Chinese. Add in the occasional American and a survivor or two from the nearby former Devil's Island penal colony, and the mix was complete. The added influence of French culture intertwined with Creole voodoo heritage infused Cayenne with a truly unique flavor.

The daily open-air market was a unique experience, and at times disconcerting. Along with exotic, tropical foods, stalls featured dead hanging monkeys, caimans, and other unusual animals that the locals ate. I'll never forget the time I passed a woman carrying two hefty live iguanas, their legs rubber-banded together under her arm along with her bulging bag of fruits and vegetables. How on earth would she prepare this dish?

Not far down the road from Cayenne lies the city of Kourou, the equivalent of Cape Canaveral. It was headquarters for the European Space Agency and the Ariane rockets that were being launched at that time. It seemed incompatible having such high technology planted in the middle of the jungle, but French Guiana's location near the equator made it an ideal spot for launching rockets into the proper orbits. There were a few launches during our tenure there, and on one occasion, a group of us had an opportunity to watch a launch from an exceptional and unique site—La Montagne des Singes, or Monkey Mountain.

Several of the cruisers had cars, so many of us were able to head out of town to this high hilltop vista on one incredibly clear, still, strikingly moonlit evening. We all sat down on blankets and had a clear view of the floodlit launch pad a short distance away. The ocean fanned out to our right and looked like a magazine photo, sparkling under the high moon. As the countdown hit its final mark, the launch pad lit up like daylight. A huge flame pushed the rocket into the night sky and then traced an arc towards the moon. Like a huge firecracker high over the ocean, the flame trailed out of sight. For a brief moment, I thought of how astounded some of the native inland Amazonian tribes must be when they see such a sight, as we ourselves witnessed this modern phenomenon from an ancient jungle.

Our time in Cayenne also proved to be an emotional and character building time for the boys. With Brendan's first experience in daycare, he became accustomed to being with other people during a good portion of the day. In spite of his tendency to be antisocial and sullen at times, he made a new friend with Tasha, who was about his age. In this new experience, he learned not to seek me out as his crutch. For Sean, it was good to renew his experience at school and the necessity of following someone else's rules other than ours at home. As much as we were adamant that our boys learn firsthand from our travel experiences, we also realized that once in a while we needed to plug them back into the real world so they could be aware of how other people lived. Then, as now, Sean revels in the camaraderie of friends, and if nothing else, a regular classroom routine gave him another social outlet. He didn't seem to suffer as the only white child in his class, and his memories today attest to that. As a special moment for them to experience together, Sean and Brendan were a part of Cayenne's version of Carnaval, as all the school children attended class one day in costume, then joined the festive crowd parading down the main street.

French Guiana offered many fascinating activities and sights to see, and on a few occasions, we went camping. Camping in the Amazonian jungle is a wholly different experience than an American KOA. Our dear friends, the Schurmann family, had finally left Brazil to begin their circumnavigation adventure, and we met up again when they sailed into Cayenne for a brief stay. We hadn't seen them since we left Florianopolis almost a year earlier. On a long holiday weekend, we all decided to trek into the jungle for a short camping trip to the village of Cacao, deep within the jungle.

Cacao at this juncture was populated with Hmong refugees from the Vietnam War, resettled by the French government only five years earlier. The Hmongs had transformed this forsaken plot of the jungle into a fertile and vibrant agricultural oasis through an amazing dose of industriousness, determination, and ambition. Vegetables and tropical fruits flourished in neatly manicured fields alongside the traditional stilt homes they had built. As they also dressed in their traditional Hmong attire, we felt transported to another time and place in Asia.

To continue reaping financial benefits from their hard work, the Hmongs loaded Toyota pick-ups for their twice-weekly, pre-dawn trek to Cayenne's market to sell their produce. Prosperity, however, came at the expense of their relations with the local French Guianan population. Since the Hmongs now dominated the Cayenne market, the market organizers sought retribution in relegating them to the less desirable stalls outside, with the locals occupying the more coveted interior marketplace spots. However, the customers gravitated to the outside, attracted by the Hmongs' finer produce.

The jungle swallowed us where we set up camp at a *carbet,* near a creek just outside of Cacao. Carbets are basic thatched roof structures that serve as rudimentary shelters, just somewhere to hang a hammock for the night. With the Schurmanns, we unloaded our hammocks and food, started a fire, and cooked up a rustic dinner. When camping in these parts and climates, a sleeping bag on the ground is ill advised.

There are too many strange and toxic critters with which one could unwittingly share a bed.

After we had finished dining by flashlight and candlelight, everyone headed for the hammocks that Michel and Vilfredo had rigged up earlier between the posts and rafters. A terrible cracking sound preceded a group crash of the entire *Cowabunga* family when our posts faltered, and the floor caved in below our weight. It was quite comical, and after the initial shock and surprise, everyone laughed. Michel and Vilfredo re-rigged the hammocks only to have the Schurmann side of the carbet do the same thing moments later.

Being sailors, their knowledge of knots and making-do with the materials at hand proved useful as Michel and Vilfredo were able to hang our hammocks one more time. Although we were once again settled in for the night, the mosquitoes, huge flying roaches, gigantic scolopends inching along the rafters, and the stereophonic noises that echoed throughout the jungle, all ensured us a sleepless night.

This was our second experience camping in a carbet with our two boys. Once during a cross-coastal road trip from Cayenne to the border of Suriname, we slept in an Indian village carbet on the shore of the St. Laurent de Maroni River. This carbet was surrounded by the villager's homes, which were a mix of carbets and cinder block or stucco dwellings. That night, as Michel and I were bedded down in our hammocks that we each shared with one of our boys, we were awakened by a low, steady chomping sound. The tall grass was rustling just a few feet away.

"I have my hunting knife," Michel whispered, although his assurance made me no less petrified. I imagined lions and tigers and bears and then…one very big, harmless cow peered curiously at us through the grass, chomping away loudly.

After celebrating Sean's and Brendan's sixth and third birthdays in March and April, it dawned on us that it had already been three years since we left France to embark on our adventure. Seven months in Cayenne was long enough, and it was time to leave. We targeted a departure of April fifteenth. Setting a specific date was our custom because, with a deadline to respect, it helped us get things done within a reasonable time frame. We had met many cruisers who said they would leave "around" a certain time and then just procrastinated. One could always wait to finish up more things, but sometimes you just have to go.

Departure day came, and we began to lift anchor...but then an impressive cloud of black smoke began to billow just as the windlass was lifting the anchor. The windlass is a device that lets the chain out, reels it in, and holds it in place at anchor. Michel had recently installed a new wind generator, but apparently, something had gone amiss with the electrical connections down below that impacted the windlass. A few nips and tucks in the wiring and we were good to go the next day. Our anchorage community fêted our departure with the traditional foghorn salute.

We had managed to cobble together some decent savings with our $5,000 windfall bonus and the money we saved from working in Cayenne. With this, we could head on up to the Caribbean and eventually to the East Coast of the United States.

But first and foremost, Michel had a medical condition we needed to attend to. He had developed a hernia, and it was doubtful that the local doctors and medical facilities in Cayenne could have helped us manage the problem. When he first discovered the bulge in his abdomen, he said it wasn't too bothersome. But after a couple of months, heavy lifting and certain movements became problematic. Our next best option was to seek a new doctor in Martinique.

CHAPTER EIGHTEEN

DEVIL'S ISLAND, FRENCH GUIANA

On our way to Martinique, we couldn't resist the opportunity to stop at Devil's Island. It is a possession of France, located about ten miles off the coast of French Guiana. Known in French as the "Ile du Diable," it's one of a trio of islands, known collectively as the Iles du Salut. Ile Royale and Ile St. Joseph are the companion islands, but in English, the single name of "Devil's Island" stuck, and has become synonymous with the whole lot.

Devil's Island was infamous from 1854 to 1952 as one of France's most notorious prisons, or "hell on earth." Established under France's colonial dominance, and known more commonly under the slang expression the *bagne*, or penal colony, banishment to these islands was an implicit death sentence. It was mosquito and insect-infested, and prisoners easily fell prey to illness, disease, and the ravages of the equatorial heat. Bodies were habitually thrown into the sea and sharks became accustomed to the regular food supply, thus ensuring their roving presence around the islands. Escape by swimming to the mainland was nearly impossible.

The island became world famous when the book *Papillon*, by former inmate Henri Charrière, was published in 1970. It depicted the isolation and rampant mistreatment of prisoners in this equatorial prison. "Papillon" was Charrière's prison pseudonym, and he claims to have escaped the prison by braving the shark-infested waters and riding the tide to shore via a makeshift raft of coconut bags. Years later, he resurfaced as a Venezuelan citizen.

It was a short day-sail from Cayenne to Devil's Island, where we anchored in the calm harbor of Ile Royale—the main island. From the highest point on this island, there was a commanding view of the anchorage and its neighbors. There was also a small hotel, restaurant, and a dock that accommodated a rudimentary tourist shuttle boat from Kourou. Ruins of the prison hospital and many of the former prison administration facilities also dotted Ile Royale.

Devil's Island itself was difficult to access since there wasn't a protected spot to anchor a boat, and the rapid current between the islands was too dangerous to navigate with a small dinghy, let alone dock one. Nevertheless, Michel ventured over by himself, making a tenuous dinghy landing on a rocky outcrop, and tied up for a short solo exploration. From our vantage viewpoint, while exploring Ile St. Joseph, we could see that he arrived safely.

As notorious as the place itself were the political prisoners Devil's Island held—notably the French military officer Alfred Dreyfus, who was sent there after his unjust conviction for treason in 1895. Prisoners deemed less dangerous were housed in individually isolated huts as opposed to the many cellblocks that we wandered amongst on Ile St. Joseph.

We spent most of our time exploring Ile St. Joseph, where the bulk of the actual prison cells were located. Buried and hidden in the deep tropical jungle foliage, rows and rows of abandoned cellblocks with tiny barred window openings, and brick cubicles were scattered across the island. We hacked our way through the dense foliage with a machete in the overgrown jungle that seemed to be growing before our eyes. The thick palm and coconut tree canopy provided us welcomed shade in the heat, and long, crawling vines curled around the window bars. There were countless prisoners' drawings on the walls throughout the complex, depicting their lives, their torture, and their despair. Many of the cellblocks had no ceilings, just barred overhead openings from wall to wall, affording no privacy from the guards who paced above.

It was haunting, walking in the footsteps of these prisoners. It almost seemed as if they had just left recently and in a hurry, as there were still cots, dirty mattresses, and chamber pots strewn about in abundance. We poked around for a long time trying to imagine such a hell on such an island paradise, but with no reference points to compare to our own life experiences up to this point, we were lost in time and our frame of minds. During their tenure, the prisoners were condemned to hard labor, tediously building miles and miles of cobblestone paths and low-lying stone walls throughout the islands. It rendered our walk-in paradise these many years later a peaceful, calm experience. The irony was not lost on us.

As we entered one huge hangar-type building, it seemed as if we had entered a living natural history museum exhibit. There were still leg and wrist chains hanging from the walls. Long, Tarzan-like vines dangled down two stories from rooftop holes, framed in eerie, veiled sunlight. There was a small, protected beach with shallow wading pools that we returned to frequently. The boys loved it. Being the only ones there, they could play and frolic in complete safety.

Numerous curious little creatures known as *agoutis* were scattered about the islands, and they were very cute, resembling something like a cross between a squirrel and a rabbit. Officially classified as rodents and related to the guinea pig, agoutis are the size of jack rabbits with a "squirrelish" face. They wandered about the island with their big hind legs, always catching Brendan's rapt attention. He would stop dead in his tracks, so taken with this little animal, and excitedly wave his little finger at them.

We spent ten days wrapped in the time warp of the Iles du Salut. Today more tourist facilities have been established, and thus the islands aren't quite as isolated as when we discovered them. But we have our unique memories and photos, and the assurance that very few people will know them as we did.

CHAPTER NINETEEN

COMING TO AMERICA

We were on our way to Martinique when—*bam*—the headstay on the roller furling system broke again, and it all came crashing down. The third time in three years. In a scene very reminiscent of our incident outside of Florianopolis, the whole genoa sail and heavy tubes crashed into the water. The extra wrinkle this time, though, was that Michel was doubly handicapped. He not only was still suffering from his hernia but also had his arm severely injured by a winch handle in the panic of trying to lower the sail, as it was wildly flailing about. At first, we weren't sure if his arm was broken or not. He was in a lot of pain and couldn't do much. For a while, I had to go it alone.

All of this happened at 8:00 a.m., and we finally inched the last bit of sail onto the deck at 4:00 p.m. Having been through this scenario before, we surveyed the wet and extremely heavy heap on the deck. The damage assessment included a ripped sail, a few bent tubes, and a broken headpiece attachment for the mast. We also knew the script: rig a makeshift forestay, get into port and see about repairs. Five days later, we floated into Fort de France, Martinique.

After getting our repairs underway, we consulted a doctor for Michel's hernia and his hurt arm, which most likely seemed badly bruised. Due to a prescribed downtime of at least two months following the necessary operation, it wasn't going to be feasible for us to take care of the problem here either. The summer hurricane season was imminent, and we weren't keen on being at anchor should such weather come up while Michel was compromised physically. Reverting to Plan B, we decided on a more rapid and truncated route to Florida, and undoubtedly a longer stay there than originally planned.

Thankfully, we had the foresight to begin the process for Michel's residency application for the States well before we left France. The file was on hold at the U.S. Consulate in Bordeaux, ready to be sent to another U.S. consulate wherever we happened to be, upon a simple request. A simpler process in those days of the 1980s, the diplomatic services transferred Michel's file to the U.S. consulate in Fort de France, Martinique within a week. Following a few interviews and a bit more paperwork, Michel was granted his green card for permanent U.S. resident status within a month. A preliminary visa was stamped into his passport with instructions that his final residency card would be issued to him upon clearing immigration in Port Canaveral, Florida.

We did stay a short while in Martinique, which was another kind of France, very different from the French Guiana version we had just left. Along with its sister islands Guadeloupe, St. Barth, St. Martin, and other smaller Caribbean French tropical enclaves, Martinique was a winter playground for motherland France, and many came from the *metropole,* or mainland, to escape the winter.

There was a different vibe here, the cruising population wasn't seeking work, they were touring the Caribbean, enjoying anchorages, beaches, and the sun. We ran into some American cruisers and a few American families for the first time. This was one of the first times that Sean and Brendan interacted in English with fellow kids on a boat. Up to that point, their only use of the English language was with me, and they exclusively spoke French with their father, as well as most of the other boat people who were usually French families.

Thanks to some friends-of-friends and former office colleagues of Michel's in Cayenne, we were wined and dined and invited along to see some of the sights of Martinique before we lifted anchor to continue our journey north. We made one last stop in Martinique in the picturesque town of St. Pierre that been devastated by a catastrophic volcanic eruption of Mt. Pelée in 1902. Entire fleets anchored in the harbor at the time sank, many of which are still underwater.

Since Michel was becoming more uncomfortable by the day, we decided to chart a more direct route to Florida, targeting more inconspicuous towns and anchorages on some of the islands along our route. This way we could slip under the radar of customs and immigrations tedium for each island for just a simple one-night stay.

We day-sailed from Martinique to the island of Dominica and anchored for the night, and were looking forward to a leisurely dinner and a good night's sleep before heading out the next morning. The anchorage in Dominica was deep, and we had a little trouble getting the anchor to hold due to a rocky bottom, as opposed to one made of sand. But after a couple of attempts, it seemed fine. Thanks to our lessons learned from our mishaps early on, it was rare that we dragged anymore. However, realizing that we were anchored on a narrow rocky shelf, there wasn't much wiggle room should the anchor shift, so we stayed alert.

There is a good, solid feel on board when the boat is well-anchored. The boat moves in harmony with the swell and stays nose into the wind. We knew the noises of *Cowabunga* at anchor—certain halyards and stays that clanged in a regular rhythm. When those noises and movements went awry, our ears perked and my body knew immediately. A quick look outside often confirmed my instincts.

We were just about to sit down to dinner, and Michel had been outside for a while, keeping an eye on things because he still wasn't convinced we were solidly tethered. Picking a landmark on the shore is another way to tell if the anchor was dragging. We thought we'd go ahead and eat and take our chances. Fifteen minutes after we sat down to eat, Michel popped back outside for a quick look.

"We are dragging," he said.

"Do you really think so? It doesn't feel too much like it," I said, trying to convince myself otherwise.

"Yes," he affirmed. "Let's go."

I really didn't want to have to re-anchor. The sun had set, it was very dark, and we still needed to finish the evening routine of getting the boys to bed, not to mention finishing dinner. Nevertheless, we fired up the engine one more time and got ready to start the process all over again.

Since the anchorage was unusually deep, Michel had let out more chain than usual. The more chain out, the better the hold. We had an additional dicey problem, however, in that our chain was in inches, and the windless groove was a metric gauge, so the two didn't exactly fit well together. Michel always kept an eye on it and helped it along as we raised or lowered the anchor. Lifting the anchor this time was tedious since it had already dragged out of the rocky shelf and all 180 feet was dangling vertically straight down from the bow. That was a lot of heavy chain to deal with for a man with a hernia.

As the windlass worked slowly and laboriously, Michel hovered over it to make sure it wouldn't slip. And then it did—not much, but enough that several precious, hard-won feet fell right back into the water. Against his better judgment, and with no time to control his gut reflex reaction, Michel lunged for the chain to keep it from slipping. He didn't have his gloves on, and his whole left hand got tangled up and smashed between the chain and windlass grooves before he was able to stop the sliding.

He yelled bloody murder. Since I was at the wheel, and given our precarious position in relation to the shore and the wind and not being anchored, I couldn't go to him. I was controlling the engine so we wouldn't drift onto the shore, and in the dark, I couldn't see what had happened. All I could hear was his agony. Only several hours later would I see the blood and the broken fingers.

We had no choice but to raise the chain any way possible. Michel's bruised arm had healed in the past month, but now he was additionally handicapped with a damaged left hand. He was able to disengage his hand using his good right one and then agonized in lifting the chain back onto the boat, inch by inch, using only his right hand. I kept maneuvering the boat so we wouldn't drift onto the shore. At the speed he was able to work, it took hours—a chore that would have normally taken fifteen minutes. Once we completed that task, Michel was in no shape to attempt re-anchoring. We had no choice but to head out to sea and hopefully find a small town with a dock and a doctor at the closest possible island in the morning. We targeted a small island group called The Saintes, near Guadeloupe.

Michel collapsed in pain down below in the main cabin, and I steered most of the night. Despite his injuries, he made a huge effort to anchor us in the lee of The Saintes the next morning. His hand was horribly swollen, in particular, his wedding ring finger, so we had to cut off his wedding ring with the available tools on board. Michel then headed to shore in search of a doctor. He returned an hour later with only one broken finger, splinted, the other wounds dressed, and a somewhat improved morale. We took advantage of that scenic spot to recuperate mentally and physically for a few days before moving on.

By now Michel was really hobbling along. We were able to continue making single night stops up through Guadeloupe, Montserrat,

St. Kitts, St. Barthelemy (aka "St. Barth"), and finally the French/Dutch island of St. Martin. After a month and a half of scooting up the islands, we bid goodbye to these tropics, and sailed out for Port Canaveral, across the Bermuda Triangle. I was apprehensive, although not about transiting the Bermuda Triangle. I was concerned about sailing under less than ideal conditions. Since we weren't able to find satisfactory parts made in Martinique, the roller furl and forestay were only holding thanks to the makeshift repair. Michel was physically compromised, and should we encounter some bad weather, I couldn't handle the boat alone. As it turned out, though, we only had a few days of beating into some annoying light headwinds—nothing too nasty.

Not far off the coast of South Florida, we passed a sailboat, and contacted them by VHF radio, much like we did with cargoes. They were headed to the Virgin Islands, having left Melbourne, Florida near Port Canaveral. We exchanged weather forecast info, and obtained some local information about this upcoming landfall port since they knew it well. It was reassuring to have such prior information.

"Entering the Port Canaveral is straightforward through a well-marked narrow channel," one of them said over the radio. "You can dock at the Cape Marina for entry paperwork formalities."

Deep in the night of June twenty-second, 1985, we spotted the blinking beams of the Port Canaveral lighthouse. Sunrise the next morning revealed a seemingly virgin coastline, graced with white sand and low-lying foliage. Suddenly, incongruent images of launch pads jarred the skyline, indicating the Kennedy Space Center at Cape Canaveral. After three years, having traced the west coasts of Spain and Portugal, Africa, the length of eastern and southern South America, and the West Indies, we had come to America.

PART FOUR

Florida

$\mathscr{P}$ORT $\mathscr{C}$ANAVERAL, $\mathscr{F}$LORIDA

$\mathscr{I}$n the morning sunlight, we could see the white pillbox form of the Vehicle Assembly Building (VAB) from our vantage point, peeking just above the horizon. A singular, lonely figure, it was intriguing because we couldn't figure out what it was and it cut a remarkable profile. We were used to seeing ships on the horizon, lighthouses, buoys, and sails, but this "box" didn't register with our familiar points of reference. Once we got much closer, and we could see the launch pads, we realized that this was the fabled VAB, a massive structure touted as the largest single-story building in the world.

This is where Space Shuttles and the earlier Apollo rockets were stored and assembled. When a Shuttle launch was not imminent, the VAB was open to visitors on the Space Center's guided tour, and often the Shuttle's iconic, solid rocket fuel tanks were visible hanging from the ceiling like large deli sausages. It is hard to comprehend the stature of this massive building. In fact, the interior volume is so vast that it even creates its own weather; rain clouds are known to form inside.

Our landfall in Port Canaveral—the servicing port for Cape Canaveral—wasn't ideal. Our engine refused to start, failing us once again and our morale plummeted. We still had repairs to complete on the roller furling system, Michel was still in pain, and now there was another issue with the engine. At times like these, I'd had it and was tempted to give up this whole "adventure" that often seemed more work than the fun it was supposed to be.

We had no choice but to enter the harbor channel under sail. The channel wasn't very wide, leaving us with little margin for maneuverability. Not keen on doing this in an unfamiliar harbor, we decided to raise the Coast Guard on the VHF radio to assess the situation. Confirming that the entry channel was not ideal for maneuvering exclusively under sail, we agreed that we would initially enter the channel under our own sail power and they would come alongside and tow us to a dock. This went flawlessly.

We tied up to the arrival dock in nearby Cape Marina, and for the next few days we were busy with immigration and customs formalities and securing Michel's green card. As the U.S. Consulate in Martinique had promised us, the authorities in Port Canaveral had Michel's green card waiting for us, and he became a new, permanent resident within just a few days of our arrival. We did a little victory dance!

Although I didn't know it at the time, this was to be my homecoming. Originally, we intended our landfall in Florida to last only a few months. We wanted to figure out a solution for Michel's hernia, a quick engine repair, perhaps fit in some tourism at Disney World, and then we would continue on our way. It turned into a lengthier sojourn, and it would be the first time Michel would *live* in the United States. I hadn't lived in the States for just over nine years at that point, and many things had changed here since I last called it home.

At the local convenience store, we found ourselves befuddled by a microwave oven. How did you turn it on? How did it work? Also, politically things had drastically changed. Ronald Reagan was now President, and I bemoaned the passing of the revolutionary 60s and 70s of my high school and college days. I was confounded as to this new society that that harkened back to "the good ole' days," where people sought solace in the homey stereotype of life from the 1950s.

What happened to the young adult outrage against societal conventions, prompted by anti-Vietnam War sentiment? What of public reassessment of our institutions since the fallout from the Watergate scandal? Adding to my confusion, Florida perplexed me. Having grown up and lived only in the state of California, I didn't understand Floridian slang or the prevailing southern accent, and I also found the émigré New Yorker retiree's particular frame of mind unappealingly grumpy. Florida's perpetual hot and humid climate was difficult to assimilate to without the countering trade winds effect we had known up to now, and the constant threat of alligators everywhere was alarming! Yes, coming "home" was a sobering experience.

We sought out a semi-permanent berthing solution in order to deal with our engine repair. Port Canaveral was more of an industrial and fishing harbor than a welcome refuge for passing cruisers, and at this time of the year in June 1985, the sun and humidity were relentless. There was no place for the kids to play, it would be too expensive at the marina, and the combination of dust, asphalt, the cement wharf, and heat rendered living conditions oppressive. We instead targeted cities along the Intracoastal Waterway since it seemed there would be more pleasant and viable living conditions along that route. The Intracoastal Waterway, or the ICW, is an inland body of water that slices down the eastern seaboard of the United States, paralleling the Atlantic Ocean and the Gulf Stream. In Florida, this inland waterway is bordered by communities, marinas, and housing developments with offshoot labyrinths of canals, their shores lined with homes and private docks.

Finding a semi-permanent, inexpensive berthing solution was proving very difficult. We always avoided marinas due to the cost, and on top of that, we learned that "liveaboards" were not allowed in most of them anyway. Finding a legal anchorage was also a challenge because most communities along the ICW had instituted "no anchor" ordinances in recent years. Cruising was becoming more popular, and there were an increased number of pleasure boats consistently plying the Waterway. As it often happens, a few bad apples had spoiled things for everyone else, and cities along the Waterway had started to ban anchoring to avoid the problems of long-term anchored junk, rowdy occupants, late night parties, and pollution.

We eventually settled in an anchorage in the community of Indian Harbour Beach. Having heard about this spot from some locals we met, we rented a car for a day and made a quick reconnaissance of the larger surrounding area. The anchorage known as Dragon Point was particularly attractive, located at the confluence of the southern tip of Merritt Island and Indian Harbour Beach, where the Banana River flows into the Intracoastal Waterway. Dragon Point was a rather farcical place, so christened for its thirty-foot long, cartoon-like sculpture of a green-hued dragon, a conspicuous and storied landmark in the area.

With two marinas and a yacht club nestled amidst comfortable homes, passing cruisers were tolerated here. An elementary and preschool were nearby, as well as necessary shopping centers, a hardware store, and access to water. The whole area also seemed to be well-protected should a summer hurricane pass through. It didn't seem like such a bad place to be stuck for a while. But first, we had to get down there, and not having an engine crossing from Port Canaveral to the Intracoastal Waterway was a major hurdle. Once through the Barge Canal that joined the port to the ICW, we could sail down the rest of the way. But we needed a tow.

After our experience in Argentina, where generosity and genuine goodwill reigned, we had to adjust to American pragmatism as we sought a reasonable solution. We were reminded of certain places in Senegal where anything could be done or had...for a price. We had numerous price proposals for a tow—up to $100 or more. In business, time is money. We could understand a small fee, but given the short distance through the canal and a maneuver that even a small boat with a simple outboard motor could execute, $100 seemed excessive as if we were being taken advantage of for just needing the help. Having been accustomed to the camaraderie and sharing mentality of our cruising culture, we were taken aback and disgusted by the greed. Eventually, we happened upon Nick, a young and generous local sailor, who offered to help with his Boston Whaler free of charge. On the appointed Saturday, Nick and his girlfriend, Eileen showed up, and in no time flat, they towed us through the swampy canal passage and unleashed us into the Waterway, where we sailed the rest of the day down to Dragon Point.

Despite our new friends' helping hands, the sail was nerve wracking and exhausting. Due to our six-foot draft, we had to stay within the narrow Waterway channel to avoid running aground. Not only that, but the wind forced us to tack (zig-zag) almost every five minutes for the whole day. We also had a quick introduction to the area's summer weather pattern whereby after the searing daytime heat, an incredibly violent thunderstorm whipped up in the early evening. The wind roared and the rain pelted. Not being familiar with the impending signs of it, we were caught off guard and suffered a knockdown under full sail from a huge gust. Our genoa sail ripped in several places, sending some unattached items on the deck into the water. Eventually, we learned we could set our clocks by the regular arrival of the 5 p.m. thunderstorm throughout the summer season.

Once settled into the Dragon Point anchorage, we found a discreet spot in a nearby canal where we could tie up the dinghy to go on land without bothering the neighbors. Finally able to tackle our first problem, we sought out a competent marine mechanic for the engine, which took precedence over Michel's hernia in the short term. It was imperative to have a working engine with the impending hurricane season. It would be too dangerous for us to be caught at anchor in a violent storm and not be able to move if necessary.

When recommendations from the local marina coincided with several others for a certain Jim Mazza, we gave him a call. Jim came right away and performed an in-depth diagnostic review of the engine, and an initial trial repair proved fruitless—as he forewarned might possibly be the case. After weighing all the options and remembering the troubles we'd had with it over the years, we agreed that it wasn't worth attempting any more repairs. We needed a new engine, and that would cost $4,000. Despite the $5,000 we earned in Fortaleza and the savings we were able to set aside from Cayenne, buying a new engine would take a big chunk out of our budget, leaving us with a meager cushion, so it seemed our decision was made for us. We'd have to stay put in Florida for a while.

Once we resigned ourselves to this new twist in our plans, Michel looked for a job. To do this, we needed transportation, so Michel indulged his lifelong wish of owning a "big American car." He rode our bike just a few miles across the Eau Gallie Bridge to the first used car lot he came across, and for $500 bought an oversized, rusted, 1970s-era Ford LTD sedan. I was mortified! Cars had already downsized in the States by 1985, so this was even big by American standards at the time. Within just a week of looking for work, Michel landed a job. One day he was simply a cruiser, a "sail bum," who worried about rigging, sails, and engine repairs. Then, in what seemed like a blink of an eye, he was working for NASA.

This whole area dubbed the "Space Coast" runs from Cape Canaveral down to Melbourne, Florida, and was reminiscent of a company town. Many jobs were connected to NASA and the Kennedy Space Center, either directly or indirectly through subcontractors. Michel worked for several architectural and engineering firms during our three-year tenure there, and they all entailed subcontract work for the Space Center. During our last year, he worked for EG&G, one of the Space Center's major contracted engineering firms, where he was intimately involved with launch pad projects, a newer generation of the Space Shuttle, and a comprehensive building code for the entire Kennedy Space Center campus. He even procured a special security clearance, affording him the remarkable opportunity to be within touching distance of the Shuttle as he followed its snail-paced, overnight trip from the Vehicle Assembly Building to the launch pad, on the exclusive "crawler."

When it came time to find work, it never ceased to surprise us that my husband's profession as a French-licensed architect proved the perfect ticket to finance our travels. He would pop into a phone booth, (pre-cell phone era!), rip out local architects' listings from the phone book yellow pages, place a few phone calls, and nab a meeting. Then, just like Superman, he would step out of the phone booth, and have a job within a day or two. Just like that. No fancy résumés, no suit and tie, no prepared interview, and in many cases, no shoes—he would still be wearing his flip flops!

As nomad "liveaboards" living off the grid, we were able to plug back into the system. We settled into the American way of life, all while still living on *Cowabunga*. I signed the kids up for swim lessons with the recreation department so they could learn proper form, we got our Florida drivers' licenses, we bought Sean a bicycle and taught him how to ride, and I registered Sean for school while scouting out a preschool for Brendan. Maybe our forced stay came at a good time. It would be the first time Sean and Brendan attended school in the States, the first time in English, and for Brendan the first time in school, period. We began to carve out our own little space, becoming as comfortable as we could in our new situation.

CHAPTER TWENTY-ONE

The Shack on Merritt Island

We soon had a system for our new routine when Michel would arrive home from work. Given permission to park his enormous car at the adjacent gas station, he'd walk next door to the marina and out to the end of one the docks. There he'd give me a shout, and off I would go in the dinghy to pick him up. It was one such evening, about ten days before school started that our newfound friends Dion and Jessie aboard *Baloo* waved us down and invited us for a beer on our way back to *Cowabunga*. There was another couple onboard that had recently sailed down from Port Canaveral, and they spoke of a curious "purple aluminum" boat they saw there.

We couldn't believe it! It could only be *Jakaranda*! Right then and there, Michel went back to the car and drove up the length of Merritt Island to find them. Yes, it was their boat, but no one was onboard. Michel left a note, and the next day Nadette called Michel at work. It seems that they were also looking for a good, safe spot to stay for the winter. After hearing our praises for Dragon Point we convinced them to come join us, and they sailed down the Intracoastal Waterway to the anchorage just a few days later. It was a grand reunion since the last time we were all together was in Bahia, Brazil, a little over a year earlier.

From our vantage point anchored out in the Waterway, we spied "The Shack," a crumbling, decaying cabin on the shore, perched just above the mangroves across from our anchorage. It was obviously abandoned and seemed uninhabitable. It was an anomaly, this ramshackle hut hugging a spot on an exclusive shoreline in the midst of an upper crust, secluded tropical enclave. Alec took a particular interest in the shack since there was a dock, parking spaces in the front, a rudimentary kitchen, a bathroom, and a huge rumpus room upstairs that could serve as a great playroom for all four kids. We envisioned "Lego Central!" We wondered how we could go about legally "squatting" there. We didn't really need to live in it since we had our boats, but it would be so helpful so have this as an annex, and a common kitchen area and bathroom would be such a luxury.

After some research and footwork, Alec found the owner of the shack, and coincidentally, also of the dragon statue. He was an eccentric, older, moneyed gentleman, who lived just two doors down on the very tip of the island. The dragon graced the foot of his seashore property, reigning over the anchorage. Alec's idea was to rent the shack for all of us. Since both boats needed some carpentry and TLC, this would give us some storage space while work was in progress. The owner agreed to rent us the place, and thus we bought a second, early '80s jalopy for the *Jakaranda* family. The Commune of the Shack was born and was the home base for our two families for the next three years.

The Shack itself was reminiscent of a mountain chalet, with rough, wood-hewn walls swathed in 1960s decor of dark paneled walls and yellow-green shag carpeting. The kitchen was thrown together, an obvious attempt of an unskilled do-it-yourselfer. Despite its funkiness and ill-conceived architecture, the Shack was perfect for our situation.

Needless to say, the neighbors didn't know what to make of all this at first. Having subtly slipped in through a back door of sorts, they were not amused. Our sudden comings and goings with two huge, loud, rusty old sedans up and down their private road didn't inspire confidence. As is often the case, the barriers were broken down thanks to the children. Two doors up the road lived the Martins: Susan, Patrick, infant David, and James, who was Brendan's age. We became friendly with the Martin family, which eventually led to all the neighbors warming up to us, integrating us fully into the community.

Since we were to be grounded here, Michel and I also decided this would be an ideal opportunity to undertake a major renovation of the galley on *Cowabunga*. Now three years into our journey, I discerned several things that didn't work properly for me in the confined space where I spent a major portion of my time. So, Michel took it all apart, and between the kitchen in the Shack and an ice chest, we were able to make do for a couple of months.

School began shortly after we acquired the Shack, and it was a major adjustment for all four kids. After some testing, the school authorities decided it would be better for Sean to start in "TK" or the Transitional Kindergarten level. Michel and I balked with parental pride. We knew he was intelligent. At six years old, he had a vast knowledge of sailing, the weather, fish, geography, different cultures, countries, and languages. But when a teacher was surprised that he didn't know what a saddle for a horse was, or that he would point to the letter "M" for house (since the French word for house is *maison*) we realized that he had some different things to learn here. We insisted on giving first grade a try, but very soon it was apparent that Sean was unhappy and a bit overwhelmed by the new environment, as well as the many things he hadn't yet mastered. After he had transitioned to the TK class, it was a much better fit.

We also knew that Sean and Brendan would have some adjustments to make using English more on a daily basis. Although I only spoke English with them to ensure their bilingualism and they absolutely understood every word, they would respond in French. We had lived in a predominantly French environment up until our arrival in Florida.

Brendan had never actually spoken English much, but I knew he would quickly adapt. Several years earlier I had a similar experience with Sean when I put him in preschool in France. He spoke more English at that point since he was at home with me while Michel was at work. His teacher at the time was worried that he wouldn't be able to communicate in French. I assured her then, as I reassured Brendan's teacher, that he understood everything. Given that Brendan wasn't talkative or outgoing to begin with, I explained that he would undoubtedly take his time before being comfortable in communicating.

By Christmas, both boys were happy campers. The drama of leaving me in the mornings had dissipated for Brendan, and they both became comfortable with English. They made new friends, became involved with after-school soccer, and learned to ride bikes. Brendan and Gougou were a great comfort to each other in the dawning days of school. They were both so similarly reserved that plunging them into their new environment together seemed to reassure them that we hadn't abandoned them.

We quickly settled into a daily landlubber routine, or as the Parisian French expression goes, "*Metro, boulot, dodo*," which means "subway, work, sleep." It was all we had originally aspired to escape, but we had many lighthearted, memorable moments crossing paths daily, becoming one big, intertwined family. We had a dock to ourselves, easy access to land, and the luxury of running water and a shower. Several evenings a week, we pooled our resources for dinner and cooked up a storm in the communal kitchen, sharing provisions, babysitting for each other. Upstairs became the Lego Room—the big space where all four kids pooled their Lego resources (a considerable pile!). They all built extravagant things for afternoons on end after school, and Sean and Jim could race down the length of the island road on bikes.

Being citizens by day and liveaboards by night was a strange experience. Michel would drive up the length of Merritt Island to work, while I took the boys to school in the dinghy by canal. How many kids commuted to school via a short dinghy ride every morning? Eventually, I found some part-time work teaching French and English as a Second Language (ESL) at the Florida Institute of Technology, and freelance writing for the local newspaper, *Florida Today*. We even gave in to Sean's and Brendan's desire for a pet, and a fluffy gray kitten took up residence onboard, becoming our intrepid Bagunça. She was with us for several years, even continuing on to California with us. Although we knew this new routine was temporary, I was still a bit anxious as to how long it would last, afraid that we might get caught up in it indefinitely. We remained determined to lift anchor again as soon as possible for foreign shores.

Now that we had made our decision to buy a new engine and were saving towards that end, we finally turned our attention to Michel's hernia. Although it had been about six months since his condition was diagnosed, he seemed less bothered by it as our daily physical sailing activity was reduced. We didn't have American health insurance at the time, so our best option was to return to France for Michel's operation. It dawned on us that combining this with a family trip back to France for Christmas would work nicely. We hadn't been back in three years, and this way Brendan could meet his French grandparents. Sean would be thrilled to see his Mamie again, and she likewise would be thrilled to see us and be reassured that we hadn't really left forever. Flush with excitement for this trip, we enthusiastically delved into organizing all the logistics. With the help of Philippe, our doctor friend in France, Michel's operation was quickly scheduled, and I was able to get Sean's schoolwork to take with us for our two-month absence.

By the time we returned to Florida in February 1986, Michel was well along in his convalescence, and things were looking up. He found another job quickly (since he had to quit his previous one due to missing two months), and thanks to a loan from my sister, we could purchase and install our new engine earlier than we had hoped.

We even became comfortable with the quirkiness and diversity of Florida. Such a mixed bag! Despite my initial bittersweet feelings towards Florida, I grew to appreciate and understand this state more, acclimating to the most oppressive summer heat we had experienced thus far in our travels. Although a flat land, Florida was lush and green, and a teeming wildlife sanctuary with herons, pelicans and all that thrived in the pervasive swamps. Nary the tiniest of ponds was spared the ubiquitous alligator. Prehistoric behemoth manatees, known as "gentle giants," often meandered around *Cowabunga* at our anchorage, amenable to the tummy rubs we gave them from our dinghy.

We were also privileged to witness regular space shuttle launches either onsite at Cape Canaveral or simply from the deck of *Cowabunga*. Sean and Brendan even marveled at several of these heart-stopping moments from their own schoolyard during recess.

Brendan and James Martin became fast friends, as we all did with the whole Martin family. For those three years, our families shared many a Christmas, Thanksgiving, Halloween, birthday, and impromptu barbecue. They were there for us, for the kids, for broken-down cars, for work on the boat, for school activities, for minor and major emergencies.

We also became good friends with Bill and Josephine Schaefer, who lived directly across the river from the Shack, in Indian Harbour Beach. As we were almost anchored in their backyard, we would exchange daily greetings across our deck and their lawn that came down to the water's edge. The teenage Schaefer boys would babysit for us on occasion, and Bill and Josephine often invited us over for barbecues and afternoon swims in their pool. They were incredibly generous with their time, advice and help, and always ready to laugh.

CHAPTER TWENTY-TWO

ℋEARTBREAK

On March twenty-sixth, everything changed, and our world crashed.

In this pre-cell phone era of the 1980s, I was in the habit of checking in with Michel at some point during his workday, from whatever pay phone I happened to be near. He was working at the architectural firm BRPH in Rockledge, again on projects for NASA. This particular morning was a school holiday, and I was at the pay phone in the K-Mart parking lot with Sean and Brendan at my side, seven and four years old by then. Usually, the receptionist transferred me to Michel's line right away.

This time, however, someone I didn't know answered. "Mrs. Couvreux, your husband seems to have had some sort of seizure, and his heart apparently stopped—'sudden death' they are calling it. But the paramedics are here and have reanimated him. He's in the ambulance on the way to the hospital right now."

I was dumbfounded. It took several minutes for this news to register in my brain, and even then, it didn't make sense. It wasn't sinking in. Michel was only thirty-seven. How do you die of a heart attack at only thirty-seven years old? Was it a heart attack? "Sudden death?"

What did that mean? It was surreal. This happened to other people I read about in the newspaper, not me.

It had been two years since we dropped anchor at Dragon Point and we were just getting back on our feet again. We had paid back my sister the $4,000 she loaned us for the new engine, and Michel was enjoying good health after fully recovering from his hernia surgery. We were putting some money aside and looked forward to sailing onward again soon. Now what? Was it over? Would we ever sail again? Would we lose Michel? I never thought I'd be a widow, let alone so young. I was at a complete loss, and my bearings were rattled. It's true what they say: Life can change in a matter of seconds.

The person on the other end of the line told me that one of Michel's colleagues was on his way to our boat to take me to the hospital. I raced back to the Shack and to the boat with Sean and Brendan in tow. Susan Martin saw me running down the road as I frantically headed out to meet whoever was coming to pick me up. She quickly called out that a black car was driving around looking for me. I very hastily told her the little I knew of what was going on. Then I ran into Bill Schaefer who was also running down the road, frantically searching for me to give me the news; I had no idea how he knew. The news was traveling fast.

Susan instantly took the kids, and the black car driven by Mike, one of Michel's colleagues, caught up with me. Speeding to the hospital, he gave me a brief synopsis. It seems Michel simply collapsed in the office while walking down the hallway. Someone immediately performed CPR, which saved his life. An ambulance on a training drill happened to be in the neighborhood and arrived on the scene within minutes. The paramedics dispensed a couple of shocks from the defibrillator paddles, and Michel was no longer dead to the world. But that didn't solve the initial problem of what exactly happened and why.

I found Michel in the emergency room hooked up to all kinds of equipment. I was frightened, and he was frantic. Clipboards were thrust at me: sign this, sign that. He kept asking me over and over again, "What happened?" He didn't remember that he had just asked me the same question minutes earlier. He didn't understand where he was and had no memory of what happened. All he knew was that he was suddenly in an ambulance. I wanted to break down and cry but I couldn't for his sake. I was just as confused as he was and terribly afraid of what would come next.

The months that followed were full of uncertainty and a lot of waiting. After a gamut of tests conducted in the hospital in Melbourne, it was determined that Michel had a very healthy heart. There didn't seem to be any disease, blockage, high blood pressure, or cholesterol. The doctors' best guess was that Michel most likely had some sort of electrical impulse or arrhythmia problem, and to properly determine this, he should be transferred to a specialty unit in Lakeland, two hours away. There was an enormous amount of logistics involved with Michel being in Lakeland and my visiting him. I had to organize for the kids and school, and find a decent car for me to use since ours wasn't dependable. We could never have managed without the Martins and Schaefers. Susan and Patrick took care of Sean and Brendan and fed us. Bill and Josephine loaned me their car for my almost-daily, two-hour trek to Lakeland. Their solidarity and steadfast support got us through this.

Dr. Kevin Browne, the head of the electrophysiology unit at the Lakeland hospital concluded that Michel's problem was something called ventricular fibrillation. He conducted test after test on Michel's heart for the next month, determining the electrical impulse threshold where his heart would essentially just "snuff out." They would electrically incite his heart to beat at such a rapid pace that it couldn't handle it anymore and just quit. Apparently, normal hearts can handle great speeds and Michel's couldn't. Dr. Browne's final prognosis was that Michel could greatly benefit from an "implantable defibrillator." Today it's a common item as small as a pacemaker, and most often combined with one. In 1987, however, it was still experimental and was a unit as big as a Walkman.

Dr. Browne couldn't confirm that this device was the end-all solution for Michel, or even whether he may or may not die without it. Michel's heart could have another episode, or it could never happen again. We could take our chances of having it implanted, or live without. Implantation involved being on a waiting list and eventual open-heart surgery, and all the discomfort and recovery such a major operation entailed. Now things were getting even more complicated, scary, and financially out of control. Our last resort was to go back to France to try to sort all this out, which we decided to do.

Through our French emergency medical travel insurance that we had at the time, a doctor and nurse from France were dispatched to us in Florida and acted in a "medevac" capacity for Michel. There were too many unknowns in Michel's condition to allow him to travel solo, isolated from immediate access to medical assistance and a defibrillator. With no idea how long we would be in France, we hoped for a swift solution, since we couldn't afford to be gone for long.

We made it to France and Michel was eventually admitted to the cardiac unit at the main hospital in Bordeaux. Two long months of waiting followed. All our notions of solving things quickly vanished due to incessant delays. There were insurance details to work out, a battery of tests and confirmations to be run, negotiations and details with the defibrillator company to be worked out, and a waiting list for the procedure to contend with. The operation was scheduled and re-scheduled several times. As in the States, this was a new and experimental cardiac procedure in France, and as it turned out, Michel was only the second person in France to undergo the operation. Our

French doctors had never performed this procedure, and there was a lot of uncertainty on many levels. We got the distinct impression they were stalling.

Exasperated with the wait, we were on the verge of canceling the whole thing. I was beside myself that despite our having done our utmost to resolve this as quickly as possibly by coming to France for a solution, we were thwarted at every turn, running into one obstacle after another. Seriously depressed and extremely irritable, I was sick of confronting the long, worried, and concerned faces of family and friends all around me. Their eternal questions, well-meant encouragement, and unsolicited advice kept me on edge. But I still had to keep things on an even keel for the kids' sake. My mornings were spent doing schoolwork with Sean and Brendan, trying to maintain some semblance of a normal routine. As far as the boys were concerned, we were on vacation being in France with their grandparents. I imagine they detected our stress, but it's hard to know.

While we waited for the operation to take place, Michel was released from the hospital at one point, but he wasn't allowed out of my sight. I became his constant guardian and was entrusted with a portable defibrillator to save his life again, if necessary. I could not physically leave his side, a responsibility that made me uneasy. I didn't want his life—or death—to be solely in my hands. I was exhausted.

Finally, on June twenty-ninth, over three months since Michel's sudden death, the procedure was performed successfully. Only three weeks out of the hospital, we flew back to Florida. We were emotionally exhausted, physically wiped out, and in deep debt. Many of our friends and family thought us irresponsible by returning to the boat so quickly and impressed upon us that they thought we were reckless for even envisioning our continued sailing plans. But we were determined.

Although our spirit was dampened, it wasn't broken. We felt cut short at this point, and that we had been thwarted in fulfilling our goal of traveling as a family and educating our children through the discovery of other cultures and lands. Our dream was now stronger than ever, and Michel and I were united on this front.

CHAPTER TWENTY-THREE

BACK TO SQUARE ONE

There we were, back to square one with no money, a load of new debt, and another health issue to contend with. We came back to find bills and threatening letters from the two hospitals in Melbourne and Lakeland, along with our two cars that wouldn't start, a backed-up toilet, and an empty fridge on *Cowabunga*. Michel was in considerable pain from the operation and not in any condition to attack any of the repair problems.

In all, the tally came in at around $35,000, which was a lot in 1987, and a huge amount for us. With no savings at that point, because we hadn't worked in four months, we had no idea how we could possibly pay all this back and still return to the high seas as soon as we had planned. Michel has often joked that although he never saw the "tunnel of light" often associated with a near-death experience, he does lament his lack of foresight in not founding a "born again" church of some kind. All profits would have been tax-free (often the case for churches in the U.S.), and perhaps we would have avoided some of the money woes that dogged us for the next year.

Not only that, but *Cowabunga* needed hull work, long overdue by now. Michel was afraid of what we would find, and as it turned out, rightly so. Attempting to stem some of the neglect before a haul-out and to assess the situation, Michel's colleague, Mike, came to our anchorage with his scuba diving gear and gave the hull an overall scrub. He was also able to give us a synopsis of how things were looking below the water line and reported that the rudder had a questionable appearance. We had to get the boat out of the water as soon as possible.

Michel was able to return to his job at BRPH, and within a few weeks, we scraped enough money together get the boat hauled out at the local marina for ten days. Since Michel was still incapable of exerting himself to labor on the boat, Bill Schaefer stepped forward without hesitation and devoted well over a week in the relentless humid summer heat to our cause. He almost single-handedly scraped, sanded, and carried out epoxy repairs.

Upon close inspection, the rudder had some major areas that were completely eaten through by shipworms, an ocean-borne parasite that thrives on wood. We began seeking a woodworker who could fashion a new rudder for us at a reasonable price, and our friend Dion, on the neighbor boat *Baloo*, grandly stepped up to the challenge. Dion was quite the artisan, skilled at many varied tasks, and he crafted us a fine new rudder.

In addition to getting back to our daily routines, we now added the task of sorting out our medical bills. Michel hadn't been back at BRPH long when they politely let him go with the excuse that his four-month absence had been costly to them. But then, as our typical run of bad luck-good luck would have it, he was offered an even better paying job out of the blue that very same day.

It took a while, but we finally sorted out our medical debts, and we were relieved that we wouldn't have to stay in Florida indefinitely. Angling to move on to California, where my family was, we finally began to put aside some savings for our departure. Despite the ups and downs of those three years, our stay in Florida was a profound experience for us all. Sean and Brendan grew and changed considerably, and both Michel and I made some very good friends, with whom we still have contact today, along with some very good memories.

It wasn't easy to bid farewell to all those good hearts and generous open arms. Brendan was particularly heartbroken because he was leaving his dear friend James. The two of them had become very close, and Brendan didn't understand why we had to leave. It hurt me that he was so hurt, and I hugged him tight as he cried. Just days after Thanksgiving, armed with a homeschooling program for first and third grades, we lifted anchor on November twenty-ninth, 1988, and headed towards Key West, our last stop before our next adventure and a new chapter: the forbidden fruit of Cuba.

Before reaching Key West, a high-powered, "cigarette" racing boat came screaming at us out of the pitch-black night, just as we sat down for dinner. Aside from the unmistakable noise in the distance, a powerful, blinding light fixed on us. Maritime law requires that when anchored outside of a marina, or away from a wharf of some sort at night, a vessel must light its top-mast anchor light to signal its location. Ours was duly lit. Thus our presence was made known.

A team of six agile men, all dressed in jeans and jackets sporting a Thunderforce logo pulled up alongside, inquiring as to our activities. We weren't sure what to think. Were they legitimate DEA undercover officers, or drug runners in disguise? It seems a sailboat anchored all by its lonesome was suspicious enough for this roving U.S. government patrol to check out. We could have been drug runners ourselves. Cautious but gracious, we bid they inspect our premises to their satisfaction. Aside from the obvious interruption of our dinner (which appeared real enough to them), Sean and Brendan saved the day. Two little tykes down below with mouths full of potatoes instantly melted away the suspicion of the Thunderforce team. They bid us goodnight and good sailing, and the scare was over.

PART FIVE

Cuba

CHAPTER TWENTY-FOUR

CUBA, THE OTHER SIDE OF THE DIVIDE

From the time of Adam and Eve, there is something about a forbidden fruit that makes it all that more enticing. Likewise, our curiosity was piqued by stories of sailing to Cuba and the cruising experience on the other side of the divide. In our French sailing circles, as well as in the French sailing press and even American cruising magazines, Cuba was touted as a distinctive place to visit with a sailboat. It was praised for its distance from madding crowds in the West Indies, affordability, genuinely friendly population, unique places to explore and discover, and of course its history.

Prior to beginning this trip and truly envisioning sailing to Cuba, we needed to find out the real scoop about whether or not we could legally travel to Cuba, and how to go about it. I first made a phone call to the United States Department of State, inquiring if it was in fact forbidden to travel to Cuba. If other American boats had gone there, how was it possible? The U.S. government cannot forbid an American from going anywhere, I was told. The stipulation was that should

Americans venture there, they were not allowed to bring back any items purchased, or be subject to a fine and the items would be confiscated upon return to the U.S. That wasn't much of a deterrent for us since we wouldn't be coming right back to the States.

Next, we contacted Cuban authorities to find out what visa was required, if any, and how to go about procuring that. They informed us that it was not necessary to obtain a tourist visa before going to Cuba, either for French or American citizens, and that sailing to Havana would be very straightforward. All we needed to do was hail the port authorities on the VHF radio as we approached the harbor, and they would give us instructions from that point on, no strings attached. Hmmm. This really seemed too easy given everything we'd understood and feared up to this point. We determined there must have been a catch, but still, we ventured forth to the land of Fidel the infidel.

We sailed from Key West on basically an overnight trip. It seemed strange to set out from a U.S. harbor with a compass set straight for the "enemy." I kept expecting a Coast Guard vessel to appear and begin accosting us with a PA system, menacingly inquiring as to our intentions. Instead, the Cuban coast came within our sights by daybreak, and we unceremoniously hailed the port of Havana on our VHF radio, as we were instructed to do.

Our arrival and welcome from the Cuban authorities was one of the most unexpectedly gracious experiences we had encountered in our six years of sailing. Our only other such memorable warm welcome was in Buenos Aires, Argentina. It must have been the Latin nature. Once hailed on the VHF radio, the Havana port authorities informed us in English that they were sending out a military escort to guide us to the Marina Hemingway, ten miles west of Havana. We weren't too sure what to expect from this "military escort." Would we be seized after all? Would there be hefty fines to pay? Would we be suspected spies? We were sure they would be brandishing guns, demanding to do a full search of our boat.

The Guarda Frontera patrol boat crew proved to be very courteous. Bidding that we follow them to the marina channel, a young man in a small outboard engine-powered boat came out to meet us at the marina jetty. The military escort bid us goodbye as the young man took over and led us into the marina channel. He signaled that we tie up at the entrance in front of the customs office. Several customs officers came aboard then, extremely cordial and matter-of-fact in their manner. There were just a few papers to fill out, an obligation to hand over our .22 rifle for safekeeping during our stay, and a quick perfunctory inspection of the boat. I pointedly asked if there was a problem that our American-flagged boat was in Cuban waters with the intention of staying for a while.

"None," they answered. We were as welcome as any other tourist from any other country.

"We don't have a problem with you being here," an officer told me. "It's our governments that have a problem with each other."

Once these first formalities were finished, we were instructed to continue to the immigration and health authorities' station inside the marina itself. Firing up the engine again, we continued briefly down the channel and turned the corner where we were thrust into a scene frozen in time. An expansive, completely empty marina lay before us. Amongst hundreds of slips, only three boats were docked, including us. Incredibly clear, bright turquoise water framed rows of decaying docks, upended chunks of broken cement, rusted iron rebar, and dilapidated buildings…thirty years of neglect.

Once we were deemed legal, Nadia, the government marina public relations official appeared and welcomed us in excellent English, pleasantly informing us that she would do the necessary paperwork to procure our legal permanent tourist visas. Nadia was accompanied by a young man in pressed white slacks, a white waiter vest, and a white apron. He sported a large, elegant serving tray laden with coffee, orange juice, water, and mojito cocktails, complete with a serving towel dressed over his arm! This was quite a spectacle as he stood framed by the hot sun and decaying cement. We didn't know what to make of this. Never could we have imagined an American marina welcoming a foreign traveler in such a manner.

We delighted in this unexpected honor and settled in at the Marina Hemingway, aptly named for the celebrity whom Cubans seemed to hold so dearly in their hearts. The marina itself was part of Ernest Hemingway's old stomping grounds, as he would set out from here on his regular fishing trips. Along with the marina honoring his name, there was also the Hotel El Viejo y El Mar, the Hotel of the Old Man and the Sea, Restaurant Papa's, and various statues erected in Hemingway's memory.

The next day Nadia returned with our visas, valid for one month and good for two subsequent renewals, thus good for a total of three months. Content that our plans were going well and that Michel, other than some occasional discomfort from his implanted device, was in good spirits and physically nimble, we were excited to begin exploring Cuba. First, we would get to know Havana, spend Christmas there, and learn some of the ways of the locals and the culture before heading out for coastal exploration.

CHAPTER TWENTY-FIVE

LET THEM EAT LOBSTER!

We set sail west from Havana a few days after Christmas, not really sure where we were headed. Detailed and current charts of the coast and harbors didn't really exist, and what did exist was mainly the property of the military. A Spanish couple in the Marina Hemingway had some information, and they generously let us copy it.

We planned to sail around the entire island of Cuba, about 2,000 miles of coastline, or as much as we could once we had proper permission to do so. We inquired with several harbor officials for such an authorization, and they seemed mystified. It seemed there wasn't any set procedure for this, and that we could just...go. This seemed odd and too good to be true. That's not what we had read according to other cruisers' accounts, and we wanted to protect ourselves from bureaucratic entanglements. We prodded them to provide us with some sort of permit or written permission, duly stamped in triplicate, should we have to satisfy some prickly bureaucrat down the road.

Most tourists in Cuba at that time were either Canadian or from European communist eastern bloc nations, visiting through group-organized guided tours. Typically, they would stay in official government designated resorts. Since renegade individual tourists such as ourselves were not common, the Cuban system lacked set procedures on how to handle our request to travel freely about the country.

Eventually, Michel established a rapport with Señor Antonio Pardo, the Jefe de l'Aduana (Customs Chief) at the Marina Hemingway. Together they set about creating an "official" travel plan. The two of them pored over charts, identifying viable harbors for us to enter, pointing out the military stations that were off limits, noting dangerous rocks, coastal outcroppings, and coral reefs to avoid. Together they came up with a guideline itinerary, and Señor Pardo said he would inform harbor officials along the way of our possible visits. He assured us that we would be free to roam with no timeline hindrance and that authorities wouldn't question our presence.

We decided to target the fishing village of Santa Lucia, west of the Marina Hemingway, en route to the western tip of Cuba. This would be our first attempt at entering a Cuban harbor with no viable chart and only some sketchy information. Toward the late afternoon, we were fairly sure we saw the two channel buoys that had been indicated to us. Since unknown reefs were an ever-present danger, our depth sounder was always on. We tried to call up a harbor authority on the VHF radio, but there was no response.

Once we were inside the channel, we flagged down a fishing boat, and they very kindly led us the rest of the way. The channel was lined with mangroves, and the fishermen waved us onward through a bend in the waterway. Not to worry, they reassured us, it was deep enough for our keel; we wouldn't hit high ground. More mangroves provided total shelter from the breeze while we continued to motor along in a still, peaceful calm. Finally, we eyed some factory smokestacks, a few barges, a crane, a few fishing skiffs, and a military vessel all nestled snugly in a muddy little cul-de-sac bay. It was a drab looking scene, yet what we wanted—our first look at a slice of the real Cuba. There was no turning back now.

A Guarda Frontera officer waited for us onshore and was polite and congenial. He briefly looked over our passports and papers, and then indicated a gate behind him which we were free to use as we pleased. As we typically proceeded when in a new place, Michel set out first on a quick reconnaissance tour, stepping off the boat onto the wharf where we were tied up. Upon his return, we gathered up the two kids and went on a brief walk about the village. It was a walk into a past, frozen in time as Santa Lucia had the feel of a frontier-era town. Most of the houses were windowless wooden-slat huts, some with thatched palm leaf roofs. There was a simple bakery, an egg stand, and a shoe cobbler, and since most daily necessities were rationed, people waited in line as we had previously seen regularly in Havana. One villager passed us in an ox-drawn cart, while another diligently transported a pig in a wheelbarrow.

Most traffic was on foot while an occasional soldier passed by on a motorcycle sidecar or in a jeep. There was a 1940s-era aerial mining tram that crossed a good portion of the village, transferring copper from a nearby mine to a dumping spot on the harbor wharf. Sean and Brendan were in awe of all of this. Havana was definitely not as modern as Florida, and Santa Lucia was a completely different reality. We drew stares dressed in our comparatively bright, colorful clothing, accompanied by our young redhead and blond-haired tots.

We later met Oscar, a young man who pointedly made his way to our dock and volunteered to guide us around. A tad suspicious that this might have been a planned tactic to restrict our movements, he turned out to be a most gracious host and a valuable resource. He showed us where and how to buy food, and gave us a tour of the local copper mine. Fifty-year-old machinery and techniques maintained the daily operations there. Oscar also took Michel to his family home, introducing his mother who spoke some English. They plied him with *dulce de limon*, Russian wine, and engaged him in political propaganda discourses on the Cuba of today.

Curiously, foreigners in Cuba could only use U.S. dollars to purchase items. There was no reason to exchange money for Cuban pesos anyway because foreigners were only allowed to frequent *diplomercados*—stores reserved for tourists that only accepted dollars. However, Michel was determined that we have some pesos in hand. We didn't know what lay down the road and he didn't want us to be restricted or hindered for any reason. Besides, traveling outside of the official resort circuit, there were no diplomercados around. Although in theory there was no way for a foreigner to exchange dollars into pesos, I learned to never underestimate *this* Frenchman on a mission. He found a black-market money exchange connection in Havana, and as it turned out, our original exchange of $100 went a very long way over the next few months.

Thanks to Oscar, we also learned that we could get some supplies in the *bodegas,* or little local food shops. The shop tenders were most courteous and anxious to make our acquaintance. We were always waved to the front of the line, and since we had no ration tickets, they wouldn't let us pay cash for items. Shopkeepers didn't dare accept our pesos since that would put them in a difficult situation. There wasn't any way they could spend the extra pesos even if we did pay them since people rarely used money instead of ration tickets for their daily necessities. Consequently, we left Santa Lucia with our $100 in pesos intact.

After a few days, it was time to move on, and Oscar was able to give us more detailed coastal chart information. Most importantly, he mentioned we might like to stop at Ensenada El Cajon, a lobster fishing station, or a *casa de pesca*. We never would have stopped there if it hadn't been indicated to us. It was a few rickety shacks on stilts, nestled together along a freestanding dock in the middle of nowhere. Although seemingly completely open to the weather elements, coral reefs broke the ocean swell, providing protection for this outstation. Since leaving Santa Lucia, much of the coast was peppered with underlying coral reefs, and thanks to Oscar's indications, we were getting the hang of navigating through such mazes, blazing our own trails. We glided up to this dock and tied up our lines. No one was around, yet it obviously wasn't abandoned. There was a generator, a cold storage room, signs of daily life, several aquariums holding lobsters, and even a cat with its litter box. Someone would surely show up soon.

As it turned out, we had arrived over the New Year's holiday, and a day later, a fishing boat did come in with four men on board. Our presence surprised them, and they duly radioed authorities to confirm who we said we were. Once reassured that our presence was legal, they couldn't have been more hospitable. We stayed several days, and they fully included us in their daily routines.

Every evening, the dock came alive with frenetic activity as big trawlers came in and unloaded their huge catches of lobsters. Once a boat docked, each man set about his duties, feverishly unloading and sorting, talking loudly, shouting, and laughing. Michel, Sean, and Brendan gleefully joined in the daily commotion, and the fishermen rewarded us with buckets and buckets of lobsters and fish. It was lobster nirvana! Food in Cuba was rationed, yet we gorged ourselves on lobster. We had so much that we even fed it to the cat. Besides eating lobster every night, we began using all our known tricks to save more for a rainy day, freezing, cooking, and canning the extra. Never would such an opportunity come our way again. We couldn't pay for it; they wouldn't let us pay for it. Our money was flatly refused.

Although there were a lot of negative facets for Cubans as they went about their daily lives, the government certainly did something right in maintaining, conserving, and even increasing the lobster population. Lobster fishing played a prominent role in Cuba's economy as a valuable export, and the fishermen were very mindful of this. The government issued strict guidelines regarding the legal size of lobsters that could be caught, the times of year they were allowed to be fished, and rules regarding juveniles and females with eggs that were to be thrown back. Consequently, there was an abundant lobster population despite the huge amount hauled up daily.

We developed a genuine friendship with the men as we settled into their daily routine at this coastal outpost. They were eager to have us try their cooking, and I would reciprocate by offering some of my bread and cake. They also treasured a bottle of whiskey we offered— a rare treat for them. Sean and Brendan became very comfortable, whiling away hours with the men, helping them with various tasks, picking up some spotty Spanish, sitting with them in the evenings, and even watching the movie E.T. with them. The boys even learned to snorkel there, in the clear turquoise shallows.

Later, we learned that we had been quite reckless when we first arrived in the area. Before finding the station, we were anchored for a day or two in a nearby shallow area, protected by mangroves. Anxious to discover the waters and lobsters, Michel and the boys did some exploratory snorkeling, mostly as an introduction for the boys. The fisherman later told us that was a very dangerous thing to do since a type of Cuban crocodile inhabited the waters, especially near the mangroves. Sean and Brendan snorkeled in safety near the dock after that.

Bagunça even had a rare treat and was able to go on land. We didn't usually let her off the boat if we were at a dock for fear she would panic, run, and get lost on land. Not only that, we were warned that Cubans eagerly caught stray cats and ate them! Since this dock was isolated and surrounded by water, there was little risk that she would get spooked, lost, or become someone's dinner. So we let her stretch her paws and explore a bit without worrying about her.

After a peaceful, enriching five-day stay, it was time to move on. We needed to fill up on diesel fuel, and the fishermen were able to accommodate us. As with the lobsters, they showered upon us, they refused payment for the fuel as well. For the same reason we couldn't pay for food in the bodegas, we couldn't pay for either of these. The government provided the fuel for the trawlers, and the fishermen were state employees. So, how would they justify receiving extra cash for fuel or lobsters sold to us?

CHAPTER TWENTY-SIX

BASEBALL DIPLOMACY

After leaving our lobster paradise in Ensenada El Cajon, we left the western tip of Cuba, sailing to the underside, or southern coast, to the small fishing village of Cortez. Not a picturesque village, Cortez seemed to exist in spite of itself, by virtue of its location on a convenient bay that was a natural spot for fisherman to launch their small vessels. There wasn't much to the town other than a short, dirt-trodden main street, and a few simple, primitive houses and stalls, yet it was all relatively clean.

Along with speaking Spanish in Cuba, we quickly discovered that they also speak baseball. Now, we are not baseball fans by any means, and Michel, being French, is totally befuddled by the sport. But in Florida, Sean and Brendan had briefly participated in an after-school little league as part of their full childhood immersion in the American experience. Neither of the boys were enamored with the sport, but at least they learned what it was, and as it turned out, their brief baseball experience served them well as passports to opening friendships with Cuban children.

Michel set off to scope out Cortez, and this time he took Brendan with him. They became quite the attraction when they landed on the beach. It seemed that every child in the village crowded around, asking non-stop questions, and hovering around them as they tried to move up the beach. Keeping this first visit brief, Michel returned to the boat and headed back again later with both Sean and Brendan, baseball bat and ball in hand. Any hesitancy by anyone at that point instantly melted away.

We had brought along a fluorescent orange, sparkly aluminum baseball bat with us when we left Florida. The Cuban children had never seen such a beauty, and they were in awe. The questions continued: Where do you come from? Where did such a pretty bat come from? Do you go to school and how? What do your t-shirts say? It was a rare sight for the village children to encounter sailors, let alone a family with young children on a boat. They took Sean and Brendan under their wing, quickly whisking them off to a makeshift baseball diamond.

The next day, Brendan and Sean were anxious to return to shore, and the children were waiting on the beach. This time we all went on shore, and it was like being the Pied Piper. The whole little crowd followed us around, and the questions kept flowing. Sean and Brendan now knew the routine, and off they scampered with the crowd of kids to the ball field. An older teenage boy took a particular shine to Brendan, giving him pointers on how to properly hold the bat, along with tips for swinging and aiming at the ball.

Since we could see that they were in good hands, and there was no danger, Michel and I wandered off a bit to explore the main street. A man stopped us and proudly said, "bonjour," apparently having overheard Michel and me in conversation. Introducing himself as Manuel, he noted that was the extent of his French, but he was eager to introduce us to his family. Normally, Manuel worked in Havana, but he was here for the weekend visiting his parents with his wife and daughter. We were graciously received in a tiny home down a narrow dirt path, and Manuel delighted in answering our many questions about Cuba as well as volunteering much information.

A foreman of a hotel construction team, Manuel proudly showed us an 8" x 10" glossy photograph of him and Fidel Castro on the construction site. "Fidel has much confidence in me," he said. He and his family were very curious as to what we thought of Cuba and why our governments were so antagonistic to each other. As the other Cubans with whom we had such discussions, Manuel praised his country, his society, and Castro. At this time in the late 1980s, it was quite obvious that Castro was embarking on an aggressive campaign to lure tourists and expand Cuba's tourism economy. Several hotels and tourist resorts were already up and running, catering to the Canadian, Russian, and European tourists, and more construction was in the planning stages. Manuel's current job was further evidence of this emerging trend.

The day finished with us buying all the kids ice cream at the village's ice cream shop (it was amazing such a shop even existed!). We still had so many of our Cuban pesos, that Michel decided this would be a good use for some of them. In true Cuban fashion, you could only buy what was available—no choice. So it was decided: a vanilla ice cream cone for everyone. It all cost only a few pennies!

Along with the wholesome outdoor activity of baseball, the children of Cortez also reminded us of an earlier time when toys were simpler, bringing joy and fun to children without the modern marvels of Lego, Gameboy, and the like. One of the kids was playing with a homemade top, carved from wax—the kind with string wrapped around the top, that one throws to the ground. I certainly remembered those from my childhood, but Sean and Brendan had never seen one, and they were enthralled. They wanted to learn the spinning technique, and the session finished with the top being given to them as a gift. These kids didn't have much to begin with, and they gave away one of their precious items. We still have that top today, as a reminder of the kind-heartedness of these children.

We didn't intend to stay long in Cortez, but we could see the boys were enjoying themselves and getting a lot out of the experience—not only for the activity but for the cultural exchange as well. We prolonged our stay for their benefit. Brendan's normally reserved demeanor melted away while he was there. He was anxious to go on shore immediately after we finished our morning school lessons. On one occasion, he even insisted that he go without Sean, and he thoroughly enjoyed himself.

Outside of the rules of baseball, we were intrigued as to how our boys communicated with the locals while playing. "Aren't there sometimes disputes as to whether or not you are out during a play?" I questioned Sean and Brendan. "How do you know what they decide if you can't understand what they're saying?"

"Oh, that's easy. They just go like this," and Brendan proceeded to make a sign of a hand slashing his throat. "Then we know we're out." Ah. So simple, the language of baseball diplomacy!

CHAPTER TWENTY-SEVEN

EL PORTILLO, A GATEWAY

After our three years of being plugged back into the routine of civilization in Florida, our Cuban interlude was proving to be the perfect transition as we readjusted our internal clocks and daily activities. We were re-acquainting ourselves with the cruising mode of living but made some changes this time around. Sean and Brendan, now six and nine years old, were considerably older from when we first departed France. They were now a huge help as crew, participating enthusiastically in the maneuvers when they could. We were surprised and pleased by their innate sense of interacting with the wind and how the boat should feel. They just naturally knew where the wind was coming from and how to adjust the sails—something that didn't come naturally for me. I needed the "telltale cheaters" (fabric strips attached at strategic spots in the rigging) to indicate the direction of the wind. They had grown up with the feel of the wind.

Despite some discomfort with his implanted defibrillator, Michel was doing well. We did have a bit of a constraint, however, in that we needed to test the status of the defibrillator battery once a month— we had been supplied with a special testing device to do this. Every once in awhile, the testing device itself needed to be charged. We ran into a problem in one anchorage when we left the testing device plugged into a random outlet we found in a cement gazebo-type structure on the shore, not far from our boat. Apparently, the Cuban soldier on duty was alarmed, disconnected it, and took it back to his superiors. We were alarmed when we went to retrieve it, and it was nowhere to be found! Michel quickly found the officer in charge and was able to explain how vital the machine was for his health problem, and that no, it was not some newfangled spy equipment. Reassured, they returned it.

We were struck by how no two places in Cuba looked alike. From the Spanish colonial architecture of Havana to the offshore casas de pesca, and the muddy bay of Santa Lucia, to the dirt-trodden main street of baseball haven Cortez. We sailed onward to the factory town of La Coloma, the white beached island of Cayo de San Felipe, bustling Nueva Gerona on the Isla de la Juventud, and Cayo Largo with its resident turquoise iguanas.

While in Nueva Gerona, some locals told us about a nice outing amidst an area of marble mountains and quarries that was reputed as a good hiking destination with the added bonus of a cave and underground stream. After our climb, we found the cave quite easily but hesitated at the foreboding, steep descent required to enter. We finally convinced ourselves to take the plunge with no regrets, entering a hidden room with stalactites. It was magical; a new adventure for all of us. Climbing back up was athletic, scraping along with our hands and feet searching for footholds in the cliffs and rocks until we poked through the surface.

Brendan was elated. "That was much better than I thought it could be!" he declared.

I know now that this seemingly ordinary outing may have sparked a flame within Brendan, mapping out for him today a then-undiscovered desire and talent for rock climbing. Today this is his overriding passion.

We had just left the relaxing atmosphere of Cienfuegos, and the colonial cobblestoned streets of the preserved museum town of Trinidad, when we spied the unmistakable red diagonal stripe across the hull of a U.S. Coast Guard vessel. We were almost certain that we were in Cuban waters, so what was the U.S. Coast Guard doing here? It seems they had the same question of us. What were *we* doing here, they queried over Channel 16 on the VHF radio.

At first, we pretended not to hear them, but it was hard to ignore their growing presence in our wake as they kept a tight course on us. The international boundary must not have been far off because then the vessel suddenly seemed to mark time, sitting in place.

"U.S. Coast Guard to sailing vessel: Who are you; what is your nationality; what is your vessel's name; where are you going; where are you coming from...?" the radio called repeatedly.

They knew we must have seen them. We stalled for time. They had undoubtedly already identified us from the name emblazoned on our port and starboard sides, as well as the obligatory American flag that flew from our stern.

"Yes, this is sailing vessel *Cowabunga* to U.S. Guard, we copy," I finally answered.

"We want to warn you that you are in Cuban waters," they responded.

"Yes, we are sailing in Cuba, and we have a visa." A slightly awkward moment of silence.

"Could you please tell us where you got the visa and when?"

"In Havana, without any problems."

Since we were a Coast Guard documented vessel, we were sure they were in simultaneous radio contact with authorities in Miami to confirm our boat's identity and paperwork. We must be blacklisted now, and on some sort of watch list for our return to the States. With mutual "over-and-outs," the Coast Guard vessel made an about face and headed back out to sea. There was nothing we could do about it now. We imagined that we'd suffer some legal reentry consequences or retribution eventually—whenever and wherever we returned to the States.

We were soon anchored in the village inlet of El Portillo, Cuba, the foot of the Sierra Maestra mountains—Che Guevara and Fidel Castro's hideout and headquarters, from where they launched their guerrilla warfare revolution that eventually toppled the U.S.-backed Batista regime. El Portillo was something out of the 1800s. Horse drawn carts and wagons crawled down well-trodden dirt paths that the locals shared with roaming pigs, cows, and chickens. Thatched-roof dwellings dotted the landscape, and peasants had a Latin flair with their signature wide-brimmed straw hats. Life was calm in this tropical bay as mangroves hugged the shore, tall coconut trees sketched the foreground skyline, and the Sierra Maestra foothills rose just beyond the main street and the beach.

It was a very rural setting, and with the mountains so close, we were tempted to try a little camping trip. The boys were old enough now to be hikers. However, we were in Cuba, so could we just up and go camping freely? It turned out, the answer was yes. The local authorities were open to the idea, and they even offered to provide us with a local guide so we could find our way to a certain spot they thought we might like. We realized, of course, this was a disguised and polite way to keep a watchful eye on us, but it was all very congenial.

The next day, we hit the trail with our backpacks and a necessary minimum of food, water, clothes, and two tents for just a night or so. Led by our guide, we hiked on uneven, rocky trails to a magical secluded oasis: an aqua lagoon fed by a waterfall, surrounded by high cliffs and palm trees. Our guide bid us goodbye, and we set up camp on a flattened patio area, shaded by a standalone thatched roof canopy. The boys spent the afternoon swimming in the cool lagoon, and we savored our evening around a campfire. It seems the local farmers' pigs and sheep also had the run of the place. In the deep of night, snug in our tents, we heard the shuffling of hooves and the munching of grasses as some of them occasionally passed through our camp. They were here first, and they couldn't be bothered with us.

The next day a group of Canadian tourists arrived around mid-morning on horseback. It seems this little secluded paradise was part of the itinerary for a regular trek hosted by a local resort. Their entourage transported all the trimmings for a noon pig roast, and we were graciously invited to partake with them. We befriended the roaster— the one who turned the pig on the spit for a good four hours. With our rudimentary Spanish, we were able to have a simple conversation, and he invited us to visit his home and farm on our hike back to El Portillo, right along the trail. Our new friend Pita's farm was beautiful and quaint in its simplicity, as many of the farms were. Thatched roof huts, earthen floors, no TV, no phone, no electricity, no running water, no access by car. Pita and his wife were most welcoming, offering us fresh cut sugarcane to munch on with coffee, and delighting in showing us photographs of all seven of their grown children. They also invited us to spend the night.

Not wanting to be a burden for their simple means, we declined the invitation. We were, however, interested in purchasing one of their chickens so we could have fresh meat for ourselves later. They adamantly refused payment, but once Michel had strung the chicken across his backpack, we snuck some pesos onto their kitchen table as we exited for the hike back. It had been a truly unique experience to be invited into their world.

PART SIX

Curaçao

CHAPTER TWENTY-EIGHT

GOING DUTCH, CURAÇAO BY ACCIDENT

Bidding a final farewell to Cuba after two months, we set sail from Santiago. Santiago had been disappointing in that it was dirty, and the harbor officials were disorganized, uninformed, and confused as to our travel authorization, unlike their counterparts at our other stops. The only redeeming point was that it was our last stop and not our original port of entry upon arriving in Cuba. If that had been the case, we would undoubtedly have been disenchanted with Cuba from the start. Having loaded up on provisions, we headed due east toward Martinique. We had the urge to go back and visit more of this French island since our stay three years earlier was all-too-brief.

Just a few hours out of Santiago, the guard watchtowers and barbed wire fencing of Guantanamo appeared over the horizon. As we skirted the bay, we thought, this is American territory…should we attempt some mischief? Under the guise of having engine trouble, we radioed the American military authorities for permission to enter, seeking the possibility of repairs. Visions of dining on hamburgers at the military base were already dancing in our heads. But they didn't bite; no friendly compatriots welcome here. We were bid to move on and seek mechanical help in Jamaica. And just to be sure that our compass pointed us in the right direction, they promptly dispatched a Coast Guard aircraft that circled overhead, prodding us along. Curiously, though, they did not question us as to why we were in Cuban waters.

Sailing east from the Caribbean to the West Indies islands was not a piece of cake. Battling strong trade winds head-on meant an uncomfortable ride with choppy seas and a strong counter-current. The going was slow and tedious, especially while sealed down below, and we didn't make much progress on an average day's sail. After a long slog off the coast of Haiti, we decided to break up this very slow passage with several stops along the Dominican Republic coast.

We celebrated Brendan's seventh birthday in Santo Domingo and marveled at the plentiful stalls of colorful fruits and vegetables that were so absent in Cuba. Makeshift Datsun and Toyota pick-up "taxis" barreled around the streets, jammed to the gills with human and animal cargo. Although we were docked in the heart of the old colonial town, it was dirty and more accommodating for small freighters. Banana Republic graft and corruption were once again part-and-parcel of our return to a "democratic society" as the customs and immigrations officials openly confronted us, none too shy about what they wanted in return for our passport stamps. We were familiar with this scenario, and once again Michel remained true to his principles.

We visited the Cathedral of Santa Maria la Menor, revered for its treasured casket that purportedly holds some of Christopher Columbus' remains. Sean and Brendan were able to indulge their desires to learn skateboarding on a nearby harbor sidewalk. Soon we casted off for the more tropical and delightful village of Boca Chica, where we spent the month of March, including the Easter holiday and Sean's tenth birthday.

Boca Chica was a pleasant, low-key weekend and vacation getaway for locals only 20 miles from Santo Domingo. Discovering the local haunts, jumping into the crystal blue water for a morning swim, and whiling away afternoons on the white sand beach were our only imperatives. We even allowed the boys to venture out some on their own to the beach or a neighboring friends' boat as they were now capable of handling the dinghy and rowing the short distance to shore.

By the time we left Boca Chica, we had fairly well given up the idea of continuing eastward to Martinique. We did give it one last try, but after a few hours of the same old battle, only making incremental headway, we decided that enough was enough. At that rate, it would take forever. So Michel set us on a different course, exploring a new destination that would be a more comfortable reach position, and consequently faster. With the new compass heading, he sat at the chart table and traced where it could lead: the island of Curaçao—just off the coast of Venezuela.

Honestly, we knew nothing about this place. All I knew was that it was the name of a liqueur. It was never on our radar. It was never in our plans. We'd never even heard it discussed as a destination amongst our fellow cruising friends. This was a curveball. It turned out that visas were not necessary, and there were no peculiarities regarding customs or immigration formalities. With remnants we had on hand from the kids' old T-shirts and shorts, I was able to sew up something resembling Curaçao's flag, in order to meet the courtesy flag requirements. Through the ham network, we were put in touch with some cruisers in an anchorage onsite, and that's how we targeted a spot called Spanish Water, which was reputedly friendly and well-equipped to serve itinerant sailors' needs.

Curaçao turned out to be a pure and unexpected delight. Michel and I loved it, our boys loved it, and we stayed for four months. Although curious and captivating in our time of 1989, Curaçao knew its prime from the early 1600s to the mid-1800s. It had been a hub of the slave trade and an important axis of the triangular trade routes between Europe, Africa, and the Caribbean. Important trade partnerships were also established with South America. A future government official in New York, Dutchman Peter Stuyvesant, was the government administrator in Curaçao from 1647 until 1664. At the time, the Dutch dominated shipping and trade, and their dominance was reflected in the emerging prominence of three of their colonial islands Curaçao, Bonaire, and Aruba, eventually dubbed the "ABCs."

Thanks to their Dutch-English-Spanish heritage, the local population today is a shining example of polyglot superiority. Simple shopkeepers, bus drivers and street sweepers, grammar school students and business owners—all are fluent in four languages: Dutch, English, Spanish, and their local dialect of Papiamentu. They put us all to shame.

Although it is a typical Caribbean tropical island basking in sun-blinding turquoise waters, Curaçao is also surprisingly arid and dotted with cacti. One of its most distinctive plants is the Divi-divi tree, a national symbol easily identifiable by its "wind-swept" profile, sculpted by ever-present trade winds. Of course, Curaçao is also known for its orange-infused Curaçao liqueur. The arid climate and nutrient poor soil fostered the growth of the laraha citrus fruit, a sort of starved version of a Valencia orange. The bitter fruit and its aromatic peel provided inspiration for the alcoholic spirit.

Curaçao is also surprisingly self-sufficient and visionary regarding its infrastructure. Overcoming the hardship of lacking fresh water, Curaçao has been ahead of the game since 1928 when they installed the world's first (and up until 2009, the largest), desalination plant which provides all their water needs. I can't confirm this, but when we were there, rumor had it that even the local version of Amstel Dutch beer was brewed with this water. It's also an attractive scuba diving destination, thanks to the establishment of the Curaçao Marine Park and ongoing efforts to preserve their coral reefs.

Living up to its modern reputation as a tropical island resort getaway, there are some postcard-beaches that serve as headquarters for a luxury resort or two. But it's the main town, the capital of Willemstad that is a wink to Holland and seems oddly out of place with its Dutch and Spanish inspired colonial architecture. Sporting bright and colorfully painted façades of Caribbean flair, the buildings capture and exude a quirky, storybook charm.

Willemstad was a busy harbor as cruise ships, freighters, and oil tankers plied the bay. The waterfront street along the harbor was colorful, fun, and lively with a profusion of Venezuelan boats, known collectively as the "floating market." There, all manner of wares from produce and fish to household items are sold. Downtown was just the next block over, where the pedestrian network of streets was lined with boutiques, shops, historical and present-day government buildings, and plazas. A bustling hub, it was animated by a cross section of multi-national people and a street soundtrack from the Tower of Babel.

Also known as St. Anna Bay, Willemstad's harbor was curiously bisected by the pedestrian Queen Emma pontoon bridge—a floating umbilical link between the two sides of town, Punda and Otrobanda. Despite being split in half, both districts interacted seamlessly in a two-part harmony as pedestrians easily ambled back and forth daily between the commercial and tourist-oriented Punda and the preserved historic cottages Otrobanda.

CHAPTER TWENTY-NINE

Spanish Water

The afternoons belonged to the itinerant children of the Spanish Water anchorage. They were one grand, wet, rambunctious, laughing amoeba of towheads, redheads, arms, and legs. They cackled in accented English, French, and Spanish, swimming and jumping helter-skelter. There were quite a few of us cruisers anchored at Spanish Water, and there was no lack of children onboard amongst the families. They were all glued together for a brief period, sudden fast friends in an unlikely paradise, with nothing to do but *have fun*!

Just a year or two earlier, a Dutch cruising family had arrived here and lamented the lack of services for yachts in such an ideal, tranquil refuge. Acting upon their entrepreneurial spirit, Sarifundy's Marina was established. Aside from providing the typical needs for cruisers, Jos, Hanny, and their two teenagers did much more at their marina. Sarifundy's was the local hangout, the meeting place, a café, the rendezvous point for happy hour. It was everybody's living room—and it looked like it, too! In fact, it resembled a cross-section view of a life-sized doll house exhibit, the front façade missing, exposing the entire inside to the outside world.

It was a busy, lively place as everyone tended to their daily chores. More often than not, spontaneous evening barbecues, potlucks, and musical sessions just began and rounded out the day. We all converged on the hybrid dock/patio around 5 p.m. or so, and added our contributions to the impromptu collective meal. A gaggle of kids usually scurried about, and an evening of good fun was always had by all.

We devoted our mornings on *Cowabunga* to homeschooling. I handled reading, English, U.S. History, and Social Studies, while Michel's job was for all things math, science, and our own program of French thrown in for good measure. Contrary to my own memories of geography being taught dryly in school, it was something that came very much alive for our two boys, simply by virtue of our living in a constantly geographically changing world. New countries, places, and landscapes were always in the forefront of our minds. Where were we that morning? Where would we be that afternoon? Where would we go next? Michel installed a small globe at his chart table and regularly pointed out the specifics of our location with the boys. We charted our position on the globe with a thin black tape. It was always so satisfying to add another eighth, quarter, or half-inch to our snail trail.

The kids were set free for their afternoons. We had no television, no Nintendo games, nor today's ubiquitous personal computers, tablets, and smartphones. Cruising kids just had each other, their dinghies, and energy to burn. We all have vivid memories of the kids of Spanish Water playing on their various dinghies, rafts, and boards. Sometimes they cleaned other people's dinghies and anchor chains in one big splashing game, and other times five or six kids would crowd onto a windsurfing board and "sail," using a big garbage bag for a sail and a paddle for a tiller. They also built forts and had intense mud fights in the swampy areas left by the low tide. This usually finished with a big group diving straight off the dock for a rinse.

We would take a few days here and there to explore Curaçao beyond Spanish Water. Shortly after arriving, we rented a car and drove
around to see the sights. For regular errands, however, the most effi-
cient way to get around was by hitchhiking. The locals were used to
casually ferrying tourists to-and-fro and were not hesitant to pick us
up. This was how we met local residents and fellow Frenchman Jean-
Marie, his Argentinian wife, Maria, and their two young children.
With much in common, we spent many evenings together either at
Sarifundy's or in their home. In the years since, we have stayed in contact and remain friends today.

Aside from the "club" evenings, we also spent a few unforgettable
afternoons rambling around town en masse as a group, exploring the
ins and outs of the alleys with all kids in tow. The whole litany of Spanish Water characters explored Willemstad's floating market together,
and in one finale, we danced in the street one warm tropical evening
during an outdoor concert in the downtown harbor.

The eclectic mix of cruisers, the unique landscape, the easy living,
the stars at night...who knows. It just all came together at the right
time in the right place in Curaçao. Like pieces of a puzzle, it was a few
months freeze-framed in all four of our minds—a magical experience
that leaves us with nostalgic memories of our anchorage in Spanish
Water that still anchor us to Curaçao in our hearts.

CHAPTER THIRTY

Andean Interlude

While in Curaçao, we learned of a town called Merida, in the Venezuelan Andes, that boasted one of the highest and longest cable cars in the world. Since Coro, Venezuela, was an inexpensive 20-minute flight from Curaçao, we made our plans for a mountain adventure. After landing in Coro, we embarked in a *taxi collectivo,* or group taxi, for the six-hour drive to our final destination. The vista of the cable car silhouetted against the mountainous backdrop, was tremendous, and we made plans to ascend in the morning.

We took the long cable car ride and got off at the end of the line, the top of Pico Espejo. From here, the idea was to hike to the locally popular, isolated hamlet of Los Nevados for a weekend stay. The only way to get there was on foot. But at the 15,000-foot level, I wasn't feeling well, and neither was Sean. Having spent all our life at sea level, ramping up to this altitude in just a few short hours didn't set well with either of us. Michel and Brendan didn't seem affected, but Sean promptly threw up. It was obvious that Sean and I weren't going to get far, so we decided to head back down to Merida at 5,000 feet for the night.

Having had more time to acclimate, our ascent the next day went off without a hitch. We headed for Los Nevados straight out of the cable car door, along narrow, twisted dirt trails. We were initially told it would take four-to-five hours, but it took us a little over six. Not in the habit of hiking long distances with full backpacks, we were exhausted once we arrived. I remember it being rather an arduous climb, with narrow rocky paths, switchbacks, and an especially long descent at the end. Michel and I were astonished upon our arrival in the village that Sean and Brendan were none the worse for wear, trotting and scampering about with energy to spare, as if they had been sitting all day! Michel and I were practically dead.

Los Nevados turned out to be a true gem. As we rounded the last bend on the trail, a breathtaking canvas opened before us with adobe whitewashed dwellings and a church steeple, peacefully nestled in velvety green hills. Wispy, feathery clouds dipped in and out, and the steep surrounding hillsides were dotted with farmers cultivating their fields with oxen and antique V-blade hand plows. We later learned that because the hillsides were so steep, tractors couldn't stay upright on them.

The village profited from its location with locals renting out rooms as primitive B&B's, or *pensions* to weekend visitors. Thus, we easily found a hut for a weekend lodging, and a "hut" it was. It was a very simple, clean, one-room whitewashed adobe dwelling, with no electricity or running water. Our only source of light in the evening came from a few candles placed on the low, rough-hewn ceiling beams, and we washed up and brushed our teeth from the icy cold creek that flowed just outside the door. In addition to the lodging, our hostess also provided dinner and breakfast for us, prepared in her simple rustic kitchen over a wood-fired grill. We ate a country dish of eggs and beans by candlelight in the smoke-imbued, windowless room.

We spent our few days there just walking around the village and surrounding farmlands. One of those days, we met a local farmer who was willing to hire out his two mules for our return trip to the cable car. We struck up a conversation, and the next day he led the four of us on a scenic tour of the area. Between Michel's and my very rudimentary Spanish, we got a basic understanding of life in the area, along with some spectacular views.

We were intrigued by the occasional yodeling-type yelps we heard bouncing across the valleys. Our guide would also throw out certain cries from time-to-time. He explained that it was their code to communicate with each other. Since many of the village farmers were spread out during the day, tending to their fields, animals, and so forth, that was how they talked to each other across the valleys. A yell stressed or accented in a certain manner meant something in particular: "I'm out here," "I'm on my way back," "Meet me there."

We met up with our guide again on our day of departure and loaded our gear and the boys onto the mules. Although the mountains, especially such legendary ones as the Andes, are a geographical opposite to our familiar seascape, they nevertheless fostered a kinship between the isolated people of Los Nevados and us, in that we led a similar lifestyle. Like us, they could only depend on themselves and made do with what they had on hand, without many modern conveniences.

Before thinking about leaving Curaçao, we had to address a new wrinkle with Michel's health. His implantable defibrillator had shifted into an uncomfortable position in his abdomen, and the battery was soon due for an update. It had already been about two years since the installation of his device, and we were told it would last two-to-three years. Since changing the battery would entail surgery, we decided to take advantage of our ideal anchorage in Curaçao and have Michel return to France for the procedure. The boys and I would remain in Spanish Water.

The operation took place on July seventeenth and was successful. I was adamant that Michel not return quickly, to fully recover and return in good shape. My memories of our return to Florida so soon after Michel's first surgery were still fresh in my mind, and I didn't want a repeat of that constant worry. Michel, however, just as adamantly disagreed with me, maintaining that he could come back soon, and all would be fine.

He returned to Curaçao on August first, much too soon in my opinion. He was anxious to return to the boat and was not comfortable that I was by myself with the kids so far away from him. Thinking of his bandages and dressings that needed to be changed daily, I urged him to wait a week or two more, even a month if necessary. We were in no hurry; we could wait. But he felt his place was with us, the family he loved and needed. So he returned.

I played nurse for Michel, but as time went on, Michel's wound wasn't looking good. It looked infected, and he was in pain. I tried to convince him to go see a local doctor, but he refused. We both tried to convince ourselves that this was part of the healing process and decided to move on by the end of August to the neighboring island of Aruba.

After a day or two in the main harbor in town, we found a pleasant anchorage at a beach farther down the coast. The next afternoon, Sean and I hitchhiked into town to buy some last-minute groceries and get things in order with the immigration authorities. We were preparing for our trip to the San Blas Islands of Panama the next day. At the time, Hurricane Hugo was picking up steam, albeit well north of us in the Caribbean and on track for the States. But Aruba was beginning to feel some of the effects as the skies became unseasonably overcast. The wind picked up, and an unusually large swell grew and surged throughout the anchorage.

The water became so agitated that it was dangerous for us to remain anchored there. While Sean and I were in town, Michel had to make a quick decision, pulling up anchor and heading to a more protected place. Sean and I were surprised when we got back to the beach, and there was no *Cowabunga*, yet I had a pretty good idea of what had happened. After scouting up a VHF radio from the nearby water sports rental shack on the beach, I raised Michel on Channel 16 and found out they were headed back to the main harbor in town. Quickly, Sean and I flagged down a taxi and headed to meet them there.

The taxi dropped us off in the harbor just as Michel and Brendan rounded the jetty. I didn't understand how Michel had been able to raise the anchor all by himself since it usually took the two of us: him at the windlass and anchor, and me at the wheel. Not only that, but Michel was handicapped and in pain. Brendan had risen to the challenge, perfectly handling the engine and wheel while Michel raised the anchor. As they slipped into the harbor, I saw Brendan, by himself, ease into the dinghy and motor up to the wharf to pick up Sean and me. I was in awe and proud of my little guy, especially when Michel told us how well Brendan listened to his instructions and handled the engine flawlessly. He was only seven!

PART SEVEN

Central America, Mexico and California

CHAPTER THIRTY-ONE

SAN BLAS ISLANDS, SWEET AND SOUR

A week after leaving Aruba, we first spied the telltale "tippy-tops" of the San Blas Islands' palm trees poking just above the horizon. This was our first hint that we were almost there. The San Blas Islands were every bit as beautiful as one might imagine pristine tropical islands to be. Blue water lagoons lapped deserted, powder-sugared beaches, and the requisite clump of coconut trees leaned just inside the photo frame.

Our voyage to these islands was calm and uneventful, but feelings of worry and mounting stress reigned onboard. Michel wasn't showing any improvement. In fact, he was noticeably worse, having lost weight and was maintaining a constant high fever. Since he wasn't feeling well, he had no patience while performing sailing maneuvers as they were painful for him to accomplish. He lost his enthusiasm to fish, for his night watch, helping with the meals, engaging Sean and Brendan in the navigation, and doing his part for school. He wasn't much help with the daily chores since he felt so lousy, and I resented that. I felt like I had to do twice as much. I kept trying to be understanding, but our patience was wearing thin.

I tried to tell him that he didn't look good, that maybe we should go straight on to Panama and forego the San Blas. But deep down I wanted so badly to visit these islands, so I didn't press the point, and he didn't either. We may never have gotten the chance to come here again. It was a now-or-never visit. We had a fairly complete onboard pharmacy, so we continued to plunder it, seeking the miracle solution. Maybe he would still get better. Just a while longer...

Home to the Cuna Indians (also spelled Kuna), the San Blas Islands are an autonomous territory of Panama and a unique example of how people can succeed in safeguarding their customs in spite of the menacing incursion of modern life. The Cunas have preserved their traditions, ceremonies, dress, and language, while concurrently bowing to some concessions of the world, having integrated a limited amount of organized tourism.

Only forty-nine of the 378 San Blas islands are inhabited, leaving many isolated anchorages of incredible beauty and peaceful solitude to be discovered. We cherished such places, because contrary to what many may think, such opportunities for peace were few and far between on our voyage. They provided good occasions for meditating upon our condition and status, taking stock of where we had been, and thinking about where we think we may go.

Despite his condition, Michel made a huge effort to do a few activities with the boys in San Blas. An afternoon dive with them and an unexpected good catch for the day sometimes rounded things out perfectly. One such catch was a decent-sized stingray that Michel caught with the spear gun. Locals had warned of roaming sharks, and all three breathlessly confirmed this after just such an encounter during an afternoon of snorkeling. Although only a brief "swim-by," it was enough to be too close for comfort. Brendan frantically scrambled onto

Michel's back, clutching at his neck for safety. Sean busied himself noting the shark's markings and telltale signs of its particular species. Upon surfacing, they all recounted excitedly what they had seen, and Sean was convinced that it was a nurse shark. Not the most dangerous shark species, but still it was a shark, up close and personal.

After our first few days of serenity and regrouping, we lifted anchor for one of the nearby inhabited islands where we hoped to acquaint ourselves with some locals. Not being well charted, the San Blas Islands required that we use sight navigation to get around. We had a few vague sketches handed down from past visiting boats, and Michel or I positioned ourselves in a lookout perch at the bow of the boat. With this viewpoint and hand signals, the bow lookout could indicate the best path to the helmsman as to where to pass between rocks and coral reefs according to the change in color of the water. The water was so incredibly clear that white sandy channels or passageways were obvious. Anything else was doubtful and to be avoided. This system served us well, and onward we weaved through the islands.

Graciously welcomed by Cuna villagers, we were invited to wander freely on land. They waved and smiled as we meandered through expanses shaded by coconut tree canopies and bordered by their simple, thatched-roof bamboo huts. Colorful laundry hung to dry and wispy smoke wafted up from their cook fires, which were usually smoking fish. Some of the villages on the islands hosted simple yet charming tourist huts and minimal facilities that meshed easily with their village livelihoods. However, since we were still mindful that this island was not one oriented for tourists, we took care to tread lightly, respect their privacy, and preserve the same opportunity for other cruisers.

Perhaps the most famous and outstanding hallmarks of the Cuna Indians are the women's handmade *molas*: intricate, exquisite, colorful hand-sewn blouses. Molas are also 12-inch square swatches of multi-layered cloth, embroidered in reverse appliqué of intricate designs and patterns that evoke their culture and surroundings. This is an exclusive activity of the Cuna women, and they lead the business of selling and trading these handcrafted items. Although reserved and often shy, the women were eager to trade or sell their molas. Several of them would come alongside our boat, escorted in a hand-hewn dugout or *cayuca* by some of the village men. Since the women generally only spoke the native Cuna language, the men served as translators and spoke to us in Spanish.

Although they were pleased to accept cash payments for molas, they were also just as pleased, if not more so, to barter for household items. A particular hit was small children's clothing, and I became quite a popular source, doling out Brendan's baby things in exchange for molas that caught my fancy. This was all a calm, pleasant exchange. No hard sell here. Often, they would just paddle by for a brief visit in the evenings, offering fruit, fish or lobsters, or seeking a bit of conversation to indulge their curiosity about us.

We were struck by how stylish the women were in their mola blouses, wrap-around skirts, beaded bracelets and anklets, and bedecked with multiple earrings and nose rings. They fashioned their deep black hair in precision-cut, spartan bobs, often topped with bright red bandana headdresses. Their outfits were always bright, loud colors with terribly mismatched flowers, plaids and whatever swatches of fabric they got hold of, but somehow it all came together, and they cut quite striking figures. I could never understand how they could be so dressed to the nines in such heat!

After several days, we lifted anchor for the main island, Rio Sidra. What a difference from the calm, serene lagoons we knew up to that point. Rio Sidra was an explosion of population. I don't think there was but two feet separating each thatched roof hut from another, all lined up along labyrinths of narrow dirt paths that crisscrossed the island. There were no lonely coconut trees, no secluded white sandy beaches or grassy expanses. All one could see was wall-to-wall, wood-plank or bamboo stick huts—it's home to about 2000 people, we were told. For all this humanity crammed together, it was amazingly clean; no trash or rotten food lingered, and no unpleasant odors.

Our welcome to Rio Sidra was equally surprising. Reprising a scene from some old movie, we were met by an armada of cayucas—a veritable assault of shouting, smiling people. They rowed and crowded alongside us as we anchored, hanging on to sides of our boat, waving their molas, and bidding us to come ashore. There were several other sailboats already at anchor, and as others arrived a few days after us, the same scene unfolded each time.

Children were like ants; they were active and everywhere. They immediately swept up Sean and Brendan into soccer games. A few of them also had an old leaky dugout, and they enticed our boys to swim and play with them for hours, climbing in and out of the old, sinking, hollowed-out tree trunk, having a grand old time.

On land, we met Daniel, a resident Cuna, who showed us around and invited us into his hut to meet his family. He also invited us to a traditional ceremonial event set to unfold in the coming days, marking the passage of an adolescent girl into womanhood. On this particular occasion, the ceremony was for two girls. Intrigued and honored by this invitation, we eagerly accepted.

A few days later, we were escorted into in a large, open-air meeting area, reserved for tribal ceremonies and gatherings. It was a colorful, yet solemn scene, with the women forming a bright tapestry of mola blouses and sarongs, all seated along one side of the area smoking pipes. The men sat facing them on the opposite side of the room. An inner circle of "wise men" or priests, clad in rose-colored shirts, ties, hats, and smoking large crude cigars, were seated around pots of burning cacao incense. Every few minutes these select men would stand and circulate around the room, blowing smoke in the observers' faces to purify their souls.

Many casks of *chicha*, a fermented sugarcane and corn drink, were consumed over the next several days, while a consistent hum of ceremonial incantations—reminiscent of Native American chanting—droned on. Finally, in preparation for the culmination of these festivities, the two adolescent girls were prepared for their passage. Two deep holes were dug for the girls, where they dutifully spent several hours sitting as part of their purification process. Then, in what symbolized their new start in life, their heads were shaved and covered with a shawl. But before their heads were shaved, we were escorted to view the girls in a special hut. Since this was clearly a sacred ceremony, they honored us with this viewing.

Although shamans had their rightful place in Cuna society, the Cunas also recognized that modern medicine had a useful role. Several of the village men came urgently knocking on our hull one evening and explained that the village chief was terribly ill. The nearest doctor could only be reached by boat, or on a two-day trek by foot. He hadn't been able to urinate for several days and consequently was in pain. Most cruisers have elaborate pharmacies onboard, and between us and a neighboring boat, we gathered quite a stash of diuretic medication along with a catheter. Michel and the fellow sailor quickly returned to shore and were escorted to the beach where the chief was laying on a table, which was elevated on a platform. Surrounded by men of the village holding a halo of brightly lit lanterns, "doctor" Michel and his associate proceeded to administer the diuretics, hoping to avoid a direct intervention with the catheter. The medication had an almost instantaneous effect, and the two cruisers were practically anointed new shamans right then and there! The irony of the situation, however, wasn't lost on me as Michel, sick as he was, still rallied to help the chief.

Before coming to Rio Sidra, we had met Arnulfo Robinson in one of our earlier anchorages on Holandesa Cay, who had a home on Rio Sidra. He found us again and insisted we take a trip with him and his son to visit a tribal cemetery that was upriver. With his son, Arnulfo Jr., at the helm of a powerful outboard, Sean, Brendan, Michel, and I, along with another cruising couple, all piled into a family-sized cayuca. The cayuca punched a hole through some low-hanging vegetation to a small waterway on the other side, and suddenly we were cruising down a peaceful jungle river. At one point, we passed another cayuca, and they engaged our chauffeur in a brief conversation. Arnulfo Jr. suddenly cut the engine. In his enthusiasm as a guide, it seems he had forgotten to respect and important Cuna belief: the spirits of the deceased send "roots" downriver from their resting place in the nearby cemetery. Normally, outboard engines were forbidden so the dead wouldn't be disturbed.

Before long, we tied up alongside the riverbank and took a short walk into the forest. A cemetery is a sacred place for the Cunas—there were many mounds of varying sizes (and noticeably small ones for children). Pots of burning incense graced the heads of several graves, which were tended to by some women. We were honored by the openness and genuine welcome extended to us. The Cunas seemed eager for us to learn about them, understanding that by spreading this knowledge among passersby, it would help in keeping their civilization intact.

My memories of our month in San Blas are bittersweet. A sweet and sublime experience, it was soured by Michel's state. One month of burying our head in the sand was much too long for Michel as he was visibly worse, having greatly deteriorated. His high fever continued, he had more weight loss, he was weak, exhausted, in pain, and had developed a worrisome cough. He hadn't really enjoyed the San Blas as he could have. It was obvious that we had played with fire and lost. By now it was the end of October, almost four months since his operation. Sufficiently alarmed at this point, I managed to convince Michel that we urgently had to get to a doctor. We weighed anchor and speedily headed to Panama.

CHAPTER THIRTY-TWO

PANIC IN PANAMA

We arrived at dawn in Colon, Panama, the Atlantic entry port for the Panama Canal, on October twenty-eighth. I didn't waste a minute. As soon as we were tied up, I tried urgently to find a doctor without success. Michel looked worse, was out of breath, and had difficulty walking. Since we were in the canal zone and there were American soldiers nearby, I figured there must be a base, headquarters, or something. Extremely alarmed, I took a desperate measure and hailed a taxi, whisking him off to the American Military Hospital. I had no clue where the military hospital was. In my panic, I just told the taxi to go there. Michel couldn't see himself and couldn't understand why I was in such a rush.

Just before our arrival, there had been several failed coups attempts by members of the Panamanian Defense Forces, which targeted the overthrow of the Panamanian strongman and dictator General Manuel Noriega. Although Noriega had a long history with the United States as a former CIA informant and collaborator, the tables turned on him in 1986 when Seymour M. Hersh of the New York Times accused him of drug trafficking, money laundering, and murder. It soon became inconvenient for the U.S. to maintain a cooperative relationship with him. Tensions mounted when U.S. courts indicted Noriega on drug-related charges, followed by the coups attempts, which we can guess were most likely backed by the U.S. We had unwittingly arrived in the midst of this tense scenario, flying our registered vessel's American flag. Antagonistic diplomatic maneuvers were jockeying around, escalating emotions to the point of no return. We were just a month shy of the 1989 invasion of Panama, ordered by President George H. W. Bush. Panama was an unsafe place for Americans, and it wouldn't take much now to tip things over the edge.

I had no choice but to leave the boys alone on the boat while I carted Michel off to the hospital, and it scared me to do so. They were only seven and ten. Not only was the military situation precarious, but the Colon area had a notorious reputation for rampant crime and seedy characters, including the wharf where we were docked. I impressed upon them the gravity of the situation—our own, as well that of the area—and that they stay put, and not leave the boat under any circumstance.

We arrived at the American Military Hospital emergency room. I gave them a brief synopsis of Michel's history, that he was equipped with an implantable defibrillator, and of his most recent surgery in France. They rushed him down the hallway, and I was immensely relieved. He was finally in the hands of professionals.

Nervous about having left the boys alone, I quickly taxied back to *Cowabunga*. Sean had dealt with a minor emergency, fishing Bagunça out of the water with the fish net, after she had attempted to jump after a bird in flight. Not only that, he had washed her after her dunking since the water was oily and dirty. I was so thankful that he had the presence of mind to act and solve the problem.

I was able to track Michel down the next day from a pay phone. They had transferred him to a civilian hospital in Panama City where he was diagnosed with septicemia, undoubtedly contracted at the outset of his operation. The military hospital staff had immediately given him antibiotics and determined he would be better off with cardiac specialists at the Panama City hospital, who were familiar with these new defibrillators. Because of the widespread nature of his infection, the doctors guessed that it had probably also spread along the lead wires connected to his heart. The only option was open heart surgery to remove the device entirely.

Michel was able to contact our medical travel insurance company, as well as his original cardiac surgeon in France, and they immediately dispatched a medevac doctor to accompany him on a flight back to France. He was in such worrisome shape, however, that upon landing at La Guardia in New York for the connecting flight, the crew requested priority emergency landing status, insisting that Michel must be escorted to a hospital in New York. They were unsure if he could continue on to Bordeaux. Michel and his accompanying doctor equally insisted the situation was under control and refused to disembark the plane. They were finally able to convince the airline that he could continue the trip.

Once his flight landed in Bordeaux, Michel was whisked off the plane via ambulance, directly to the hospital. The first priority was to stabilize him and rid him of the septicemia. It took several weeks to bring him back from the brink before an operation could even be contemplated.

When I had left Michel at the emergency room, I had to turn to our current predicament—the imminent outbreak of war. I had to get the boys, myself, and our boat out of Panama immediately. Americans were now persona non-grata in Panama, and the only option I saw was to get through the canal to the Pacific Ocean and sail up to Costa Rica. There we could safely leave the boat and travel to either France or California if necessary. Theoretically, the canal was no man's land, kind of a "DMZ"—demilitarized zone. It should have been safe for us to travel through.

I couldn't let on to the boys how desperate and dangerous our situation was, and how scared I was. I tried to maintain a matter-of-fact attitude and tackle our hurdles one at a time. We would have to go through the Panama Canal without our captain, and having no confidence in being the captain myself, I had to hire someone. Thanks to our ham radio contacts, I found a cruiser who had recently passed through the canal and was willing to come back and guide us through for the price I offered.

With our cash-on-hand diminishing, I needed to draw from our savings account to pay for the canal passage, as well as to have some money for the near future. In the dated age of 1989, ATM machines and debit cards didn't exist. My dad usually handled the transfers of our money from our account to wherever we were. But due to the political upheaval, wiring money from the U.S. to Colon was very problematic. I knew I could count on my dad to come up with a solution, and he certainly did. Thanks to his American Express card, he was able to have a courier dispatched to me right at the dock. The courier personally handed me a simple white envelope with a good bundle of cash in it. What a relief!

Then a ten-day preparation marathon began. To start the process for the transit, I had to fill out umpteen papers of this and that in duplicate and triplicate at the Canal administration office, along with paying the $100 transit fee. Then, there were many logistics to tend to for the two-day crossing. We were required to have four line handlers and four 100-foot dock lines. Two of the line handlers would handle the lines from our deck, while two would be stationed alongside on the wharf to control the boat. A specially appointed canal pilot was also required on board for both days of the crossing. Since we would spend the night anchored at the halfway point in Gatun Lake, the line handlers were also expected to spend the night with us on *Cowabunga*. Including my hired captain, the boys and me, the canal pilot, and the extra line handlers, I had quite a few groceries to buy. I also had to organize sleeping arrangements for our extra overnight guests, repair some of our sails for the trip up to Costa Rica, and find a supply of kerosene for our stove.

For some reason, there was a very limited supply of kerosene available in Panama, and the only way I could acquire any was through the black-market trade. I eventually made a connection, and a couple of gallons were being held for me at a sketchy bar in Colon—a real dive. Walking around Colon with a wad of cash was not advisable, let alone being a woman alone, but I had no choice. In a cloak-and-dagger type scene, I found the establishment. It was dark inside and not only was I the only woman there, but I was also the only white person. On top of that, I had about $100 hidden in my bra to pay for "the goods." Following my instructions, I inquired at the bar after the person whose name I was given. With all eyes in the room on me, I was led into the back room as I carried my two empty jerrycans to be filled. I was extremely uncomfortable, and resentful and angry at Michel for what I perceived as his having put me in this situation. The handoff and money exchange went well, however, and I hurried back on foot to the boat as fast as I could, considering I was laden with two gallons of smelly kerosene. Another hurdle overcome.

During the prep period, the kids were unhappy, and my patience was wearing thin. It was hot, humid, and I often had to leave them alone while handling these details. I understood that it wasn't fun for them, but I couldn't take any time to bring them to a beach or park. They fought, and I yelled at them.

I was extremely grateful, however, that with divine foresight a few months earlier, Michel had shown Sean all that needed to be done to prepare *Cowabunga* for passage through the Panama Canal. He knew about the four 100-foot lines, how and where to tie them up, the tools he may or may not need and how to use them, how to take our bike apart, where to stow our on-deck items, and many other details. While I was running around Colon and the Panama Canal offices tending to paperwork, grocery shopping, etc., Sean and Brendan (when he was able) practically prepared the entire boat themselves. I couldn't have done it without them.

Meanwhile, we got daily updates on Michel's condition through our ham radio. My ham contact had established a regular correspondence time with someone in France. This person spoke with either Michel in the hospital, or his parents, and stayed apprised of the situation. At an appointed radio time, my contact would relay this information to me. During all of my preparations, they were still trying to get his septicemia under control; it had reached an advanced and dangerous level.

At 8:30 a.m. on November second, all systems were a go as the line handlers and the canal pilot arrived on board. A huge freighter was going to go through with us, just feet ahead. We rafted up alongside a fishing trawler, which was rafted up to a tugboat, and two other sailboats were also added to the mix. Within the first fifteen minutes, as the first lock filled, we were already elevated far above the Caribbean, which was visible in the distance from the back of our boat.

That evening, we all ate in the cockpit, peacefully anchored in Gatun Lake. With the excitement of going through the canal, the boys and I briefly forgot the drama of our personal situation, and we spent a nice, lighthearted day in the company of the line handlers, the pilot, and our captain. The next day the transit continued flawlessly, and by the afternoon of November third, we slid out of the last lock in Balboa and into the Pacific Ocean—a first for *Cowabunga*, having been "born and bred" in France and the Atlantic Ocean.

This wasn't how it was supposed to happen, though. Michel and I had often talked about the exciting event of transiting the Panama Canal on our trip. He wasn't with us. He had missed it. I had such mixed emotions. I was sad that he wasn't with us to share this moment, but I was still so furious with him that I was seething. I kept thinking that all this drama could have been avoided if he had stayed a while longer in France. He may have still contracted the infection, but at least it would have been detected early on and stopped. I was also angry with myself that I hadn't insisted more and refused to let him return early. We were both to blame, but I was still bitter!

We island-hopped under the tutelage of our hired captain for the next ten days, heading north to Costa Rica and putting Panama well in our wake. We finally set our anchor in the calm and protected bay of Golfito, Costa Rica, on November fourteenth. Our captain caught up with another cruising boat in Golfito on its way to Panama and sailed back the very next day.

I tried to put the hard memories of Panama behind me, but the situation returned to the forefront of my mind shortly before Christmas. On December twentieth, the Americans made good on their threats and launched the invasion. We were glued to the ham radio as acquaintances still in Colon and Balboa were now trapped. They recounted scenes of Panamanian soldiers taking refuge and holding hostages on some of the sailboats, outbreak of gunfire, fires, grenade explosions, and rampant looting and chaos. Some of it was along the very wharf where we had been tied up, and I felt vindicated and hugely relieved that I had been so insistent we leave.

There were even a few tense days in Golfito, which was close to the Panamanian border. It seemed the nearest border town of David was a Noriega stronghold, and Costa Rica posted guards just in case the dictator general attempted to slip into Costa Rica. At least now we were out of harm's way, in a safe country. I got back to the business of homeschooling the kids, and we waited.

CHAPTER THIRTY-THREE

GOLFITO, AT A CROSSROADS

We waited for Michel to return to *Cowabunga*. We waited in Golfito while settling into a routine of school and regular ham radio sessions. Similar to Sarifundy's Marina in Curaçao, we frequented the Jungle Club, a cruiser hangout headquarters just a short distance away on the shore. They provided some postal, communication, and laundry services, along with a basic café. There was also a large grassy area along the beach giving Sean and Brendan plenty of room to run around and play.

The town was a short walk from the anchorage, and I could easily buy groceries and other necessities there. From the deck of *Cowabunga*, we were entertained by a constant kaleidoscope of wild toucans' fluorescent yellow, green, and orange beaks. They flitted in and out of the luscious jungle canopy that framed our view of the shore, spanning the entire cozy horseshoe bay. The mornings brought a din of curious and unfamiliar jungle screeches and calls. Nighttime whistles, cries, and an occasional, animalistic shriek waxed with the sunset.

After the distress of the December twentieth invasion in Panama, Sean, Brendan, and I spent a pleasant and quiet Christmas on *Cowabunga*. We also attended some festivities on land at the Jungle Club with some of the other cruisers. It had taken several weeks for Michel to stabilize and recover from the septicemia, but at that point he was at home with his parents, recovering after his initial stay in the hospital and some surgery for his condition. He was slated to join us on January third, but some follow-up tests revealed something worrisome under his heart, necessitating another operation shortly thereafter. It would be his third in six months. By this time, Michel and I had had it with the whole defibrillator experiment, and we opted to have it removed once and for all. We were willing to live with the risk of him foregoing that safeguard. It was cumbersome, uncomfortable, and not a practical solution. Over thirty years later, he is still alive and well, and has never had another bout of "sudden death."

However, for this next operation, Michel insisted that the boys and I return to France. I didn't want to go. I was mentally exhausted and wasn't up to making that long trip for a third time in four years. All by myself, I would have to corral the boys and their belongings, their school work, prepare the boat for a long absence, find someone to take care of Bagunça and keep an eye on the boat. Then the voyage itself would be long and tedious. I would have to confront all those long, concerned faces of friends and family while maintaining life as usual with Sean and Brendan. I didn't want to see anybody, and I didn't want to talk to anybody. I didn't want to have to explain our life choices and his health mishaps—again.

Michel and I argued at length about it over the phone from the Jungle Club. I offered to send Sean and Brendan to my parents in California, and I would come by myself to Bordeaux. Michel refused the idea, and I was furious. Only years later did I find out that it was actually the surgeon who insisted we should all come since he wasn't sure

Michel would survive this surgery. Eventually, I relented, and all three of us went back to France for a month.

Sean, Brendan, and I returned mid-February of 1990 to Golfito, and again we waited for Michel. He finally rejoined us on the boat in March, four months after his evacuation from Panama. At this juncture in our travels and our life on *Cowabunga*, we had reached a crossroads.

It was time for us to take a hard look at things. For the past three or four years, Michel's health issues had dogged us. We were spent. Sean and Brendan were now eleven and eight, and money was running low again. Although homeschooling was going quite well and the experience was enriching for all of us, I recognized my shortcomings as a teacher. I seriously doubted that I could continue in this role. Also, *Cowabunga* was beginning to shrink for two growing boys. And for better or worse, Sean and Brendan would have to experience some of the "real" world, along with some of the things that were habitual to other kids in school like waiting in line, school assignment instructions, school activities, babysitters, time constraints, etc.

Targeting an eventual landfall in Bodega Bay, just north of San Francisco where my parents lived, seemed like an immediate and attainable goal. Bodega Bay was a well-protected harbor, it was near family, and the possibility of finding jobs and putting the kids in school was attractive. Thus, we prepared to head up the coast of Central America and Mexico, planning to re-enter the U.S. in San Diego.

In order to head up the Pacific Coast in the spring or summer, the best tactic is to head west to the open ocean and Hawaii, and then make one long angled reach back to California. By following this sage advice, one could avoid tedious tacking up the whole length of the coast, and a constant battle with the summer headwinds. However, we decided to disregard this widely-accepted rule with the idea of making as many short day-sail trips as possible and visit as much of the coast as we could. This plan would also hopefully make it easier on

Michel physically since he was still very thin and weak, while also minimizing the risk of being out in the open ocean should something
happen to him. I regretted not being able to visit more of Costa Rica
and some of their famous national parks and nature preserves, but after
four months here already, and with looming weather constraints from
the impending hurricane season, we pressed onward. We also wanted
to put the recent bitter times behind us.

We sauntered up along the green tropical coast and white, sandy
beaches of Costa Rica. Then the landscape transitioned into the striking coastline of Nicaragua's occasionally active volcanoes that jabbed
at the sky. We also maintained a healthy respect for the possible advent
of the fabled Papagayo winds. The Gulf of Papagayo was known to
spawn abrupt gale force squalls in response to certain atmospheric conditions. We didn't need any more drama!

Then, off the coast of El Salvador, we had an alarming encounter
with a small gunboat patrol, manned by very young men in ragged
street clothes who brandished assault weapons. They insisted on
boarding us for an inspection. Governments were unsettled in these
parts, and things could have turned ugly in a snap. We had heard and
read stories of such "inspections" where drugs were planted then
"found," and all the surreal terror that ensued. And so, we insisted
that we were just a family heading home and refused. Quickly sum-
moning Sean and Brendan to appear on deck, this seemed to appease
these military wannabes, and they quickly changed their tune, waving
us on our way.

The coast of Guatemala slid by, and we made an official port entry
in Puerto Madero, Mexico. Having grown up in Southern California,
yet never having had the opportunity to venture this far south, I felt
like I was almost home. Since the politics of Mexico at the time were-
n't as volatile as Wethat of Nicaragua, El Salvador, or Guatemala, we
knew we could linger a bit, so we did. In Puerto Madero, we met a

young man on a neighboring boat who told us about some obscure Mayan ruins in the nearby city of Tapachula. The next day, we all boarded a bus in town and headed out that way.

Once in Tapachula, someone pointed us in the direction of a pick-up for the group taxi that would take us in the direction we needed. We were dropped off at a nondescript dirt crossroads, and the taxi driver told us to head down an adjacent dirt path as if we were going to someone's hut. We went down a muddy trail, into the overgrown brush, past some peasant dwellings, then finally emerging into a clearing, we were suddenly amongst Easter Island-type statues with distinct, pyramid-shaped peaks, covered with earth and vegetation. Some were haphazardly excavated, most not, and a few moss-covered stone steps appeared here and there. At first, it just seemed to be overgrown hillsides, but upon closer inspection, the forms were too geometrically perfect to be a random creation of nature. We were absorbed by the scene, poking around the site for the afternoon, and wondering why there wasn't any archeological work going on. There must have been some amazing treasures hidden there. We headed back to *Cowabunga* late in the day.

Onward we sailed. One late afternoon, as the sun was angling low on the Pacific horizon, we spied some interesting contemporary buildings near the village of Huatulco. We pulled out the binoculars for a closer look to see what was undoubtedly a vacation resort. Then we noticed a high-powered zodiac speeding toward us. A couple of young, tan, athletic men were onboard, and they hailed us with big smiles. They came alongside and spoke French, saying they were from the Club Med at Huatulco. From the shore, they could see that we were flying both American and French flags in our rigging. They beckoned us to join them. Never having been to a Club Med, we hesitated but changed course and anchored in the bay, spending a week as special, invited guests in this make-believe world of fun and games. It wasn't our style or usual idea of a vacation, but hey, we were invited and ended up enjoying this spontaneous occasion.

It proved to be a good interlude to soothe our ruffled souls. The staff bid us partake of the meals, the shows, the activities, and as extra bonuses, they filled our coffers with French bread, pastries, and all kinds of food. Sean and Brendan had a great time participating in their games, water sports, and evening shows. The whole staff was extremely generous and hospitable.

While there, we came across three Australian sailors who had the curious mission of repairing and reconstructing the boat, *Stars and Stripes*, an American catamaran (two-hulled boat) that won the 1988 high stakes international America's Cup racing challenge against New Zealand in San Diego. A prosperous Mexican yachtsman had purchased the boat and relocated it to a back bay of Huatulco, where these three expats were reconstructing it. They had a setup of containers, rigging equipment, apparatuses, a sewing machine, and all manner of precision tools in a base station they dubbed The Kangaroo Yacht Club. The *Stars and Stripes* had initiated a revolutionary twist in the America's Cup design as it had a winged mast, or hard sail. We spent a few hours with them as they gave us an extensive tour of the boat, and even generously repaired our genoa sail that had sustained some damage from a hefty gust a few days earlier.

Bidding adieu to all our newfound friends and a week of fantasy and relaxation, we continued northbound with some quick stops in Acapulco, Bahia de Navidad, and Puerto Vallarta. My childhood terra firma of California seemed even closer now as we traversed the Sea of Cortez to Cabo San Lucas, Baja California. I realized that we had crossed a threshold. The constant warm temperature of tropical ocean water had been our familiar environment for all these years, from Africa to South America, Florida, the Caribbean and Central America. We sailed in it, used it, swam in it, and well...lived with it. But I had the sudden realization that I had taken all that for granted when I doused myself with a bucket of water while washing up at the end of the day. My lungs seized up with the icy surprise! It was jarring, and consequently today, twenty-seven years later, I still refuse to bathe in the cold Pacific Ocean that is only thirty minutes from our home.

Progressing northbound along the desert-landscaped, cactus-pock-marked coast of Baja, bountiful sea life kept popping up around us. Thanks to Sean's well-honed fishing techniques, he had good luck catching some bonito and dorado, while whales and seals would regularly break the surface. On one occasion, a whale shark lingered nearby, and a huge sea turtle meandered around every once in a while.

An oft-told tale in sailing lore tells of a sunset phenomenon at sea known as the Green Flash. It's an optical phenomenon that occurs when particular atmospheric conditions allow for a prism-like state that refracts the sun's rays into separate colors just as the sun sets. With a perfectly clear horizon, a calm, flat sea, and just the right amount of a glorious red glow as the sun dips below the waterline, there is a sudden, barely discernible *poof*, and a tiny green mushroom cloud leaps up as the last red-yellow sliver of the sun disappears. All four of us witnessed this elusive effect—not once, but twice—off the coast of Mexico. Like our vision of the mirage some years earlier, we can vouch that the Green Flash is not a myth.

Onward past Turtle Bay, Isla Cedra, Isla San Martin, Ensenada, and Tijuana we trekked, finally making our U.S. landfall in San Diego just days before the Fourth of July, 1990. Arriving back in the States was bittersweet. I was relieved to be in a safer place given our hobbled status, but sad at the same time. We didn't talk about it, but we knew that the route before us was most likely the last stretch of our ten-year journey. We officially entered the country, completed the customs and immigration formalities, and then I phoned "home."

CHAPTER THIRTY-FOUR

ACCIDENTALLY HOME

Dad answered the phone. I'll never forget the emotion in his voice. I don't think he believed we'd get out of Panama alive or really ever be within striking distance of them after all these years on distant shores. We had arrived in San Diego, and he couldn't believe it. My dad was a fairly stoic guy, influenced by the 1950s when dads were supposed to be the disciplinarian, and show no sign of tender feelings. But his voice cracked with my phone call, and it touched me.

It was an emotional reunion with my parents. After the roller coaster ride we'd been through the past six months, I felt as if I could safely unload so much weight from my shoulders. They gently prodded us to know what our next steps would be, and we vaguely alluded to living on the land for a while, not quite yet knowing ourselves what we'd do. We decided that my parents would take Sean and Brendan with them while Michel and I would sail by ourselves for this final stretch. It would be the first time we sailed without the boys since before Sean was born. We knew it could be unpleasant sailing up the coast while beating into the wind and cold fog, so this seemed like it would be a good opportunity for Sean and Brendan to spend some time with their grandparents.

I also thought it would be a good thing for Michel and me to have some time alone, something we hadn't had in a long time. We needed to discuss immediate future plans. Up to this point, we had always lived on *Cowabunga,* even while working on land. I wasn't keen on staying on the boat through the cold, Northern California winter months, and I really needed to get away from being responsible for everything for a while. Perhaps my biggest issue was that I didn't trust Michel's health anymore. I wanted to be somewhere stable for a while, just in case. I wasn't willing or ready to give up our adventure or stop sailing, but I needed a break so we could get steady on our feet again.

We spent about ten days in San Diego decompressing and preparing for this next leg of the trip. We were docked on a guest dock near the San Diego Yacht Club, which at that time had the distinction of being the home for the America's Cup trophy. Having been the host yacht club for the most recent America's Cup race in 1988, the trophy was on exhibit on the premises. Some of past America's Cup (AC) boats were also in the harbor, used for day trip outings on the bay for special guests and some high-profile yacht club members. One boat in particular, Heart of America, from a former AC challenger campaign was docked near us. It was a magnet for Sean. He was absolutely smitten with this vessel, an actual America's Cup boat.

When he learned that it took people out for "joyrides," he simply planted himself on the dock alongside the boat for hours on end. All day long, he sustained this refrain as soon as the skipper appeared. "Can I go out with you...Can I go too...please...Can I go...I really would like to go out..."

He would just stand, sit, stay glued to that spot for hours, unrelenting. Sean was 11, and the first reaction of the skipper was to brush him off. "I'd like to take you, but you're too young."

By day two or three, the skipper started to cave. He asked us what we thought. We knew that Sean was water safe and quite capable onboard. Finally seeing that this would be the thrill of his life, they took Sean out with them one afternoon, and even put him on as one of the grinders on a big winch. He was ecstatic, and the skipper was impressed. Sean never forgot this experience.

Sean and Brendan hit the highway with my parents bound for Bodega Bay, while Michel and I cast off for Marina del Rey, Los Angeles. We visited with my sister, along with my uncle and grandmother who all lived in the area. Cojo Bay near Santa Barbara was our final stop in Southern California, anchoring for the night just off Point Conception, before penetrating the ominous thick wall of fog that hung in the near distance. It was an eerie and curious sight, the summer fog phenomenon. It was a gray, cottony, opaque iron curtain just marking time, hovering in a set spot. We anchored under a warm summer sunset, enjoyed a beer, and contemplated this curtain that undulated just a few hundred feet away that would swallow us whole the next morning. The next morning at sunrise, the wall was still there. We basked in our last rays of warmth, bid goodbye to summer, and—as if stepping through the looking glass—we were sucked through the wall. *Cowabunga*'s bow punched through the cotton, and with a vacuum-sealed *slurp,* it closed behind our stern.

It was slow going heading up the coast as we dueled the current and the headwinds. Tacking, tacking, tacking—making only incremental progress most days. We would pull a long tack out west to the open sea for several hours, only to backtrack east to the coast, trying to sail into the wind as close as possible while attempting to maintain some speed. At the end of a full day's work, we had tallied up a pitiful number of advanced miles. We were sailing uselessly in huge squares, like a checkerboard. All that effort for naught. And it was cold.

At one point, we couldn't shake the distant landmark of San Simeon's Hearst Castle. It mounted the guard all day long. Thinking we had made some good progress that night, our spirits were dashed when it still stood proudly before us at daybreak. Eventually, we reached Monterey and decided to get off the merry-go-round, taking a break for a day or two.

We hoped against hope as we left Monterey that we could fulfill our longtime dream of sailing under the Golden Gate Bridge, and anchor for a day or two in the San Francisco Bay. But here, too, we were thwarted when the fog was impossibly pea-soupish. Michel's navigation by sextant was still on-target. However, it was useless in the dead of night when we arrived, and in the fog. By following the figures popping up on our depth sounder, we could visualize how we were situated in relation to the coast. We could hear the cargo vessels booming their fog horns all around us. Not reassured and wanting to be seen, we promptly notified the Coast Guard via Channel 16 of our presence in the area. They had spotted us on their radar as did the surrounding traffic, in their version of air traffic control.

"We are tracking you, *Cowabunga*," they responded, and then gave us a heads up to stay our course while keeping a lookout for a freighter that would appear very shortly off our stern. Suddenly, a huge bow appeared through the fog alongside us, blasting its fog horn in acknowledgement of our presence.

Greatly disappointed, we kept on our northerly course, bypassing San Francisco. With our compass heading fixed on what Michel estimated should be Pt. Reyes, Bodega Bay would be just around the bend. The intermittent blinks of the Pt. Reyes lighthouse pierced the thick fog in the early pre-dawn hours. It was a relief to count the allotted seconds between the pulses, confirming not only that it was the right lighthouse, but also verifying our dead-reckoned position. Taking into account the miles logged, the current, the wind, and tying in the depth sounder and compass readings, Michel calculated an educated guess as to our position. Now, with this firm identification of the lighthouse, we established a clear chart position to give the coastal rocky outcroppings a wide berth.

At daybreak, we sighted Bodega Bay in the haze. The wind was cooperating, so it wasn't too much of a tacking duel for this final stretch. Rounding the jetty, I wondered where my parents' house was, having never been to their new retirement digs. They said they were perched above the bay. We gazed upon the new landscape for the first time and soon pulled into the Spud Point Marina on July twenty-seventh, 1990.

My parents, the boys, and my brother and his wife surprised us, all waiting at the guest dock where we pulled in. They spotted us sailing into the channel from their living room window and had plenty of time to mount an official welcoming committee in the harbor. Our reunion was emotional. Eight years, four continents, two oceans, several seas, myriad islands, good fortune and misfortune, and now here with pre-adolescent eight and eleven-year-old boys, me at thirty-six and Michel at forty-one. We had arrived safe and sound, all of us older, maybe a tad wiser, and with few regrets.

In rapid succession, we found jobs, bought another vintage "tank," an old 1966 Ford station wagon that Michel fell in love with (plus it was all we could afford), rented a quaint wooden cabin in the redwood hamlet of Occidental, got the boys sorted out for school in the fall, and hauled out *Cowabunga* for hull cleaning and maintenance.

As with our previous long-term stops in Cayenne and Florida, we put the boys in school for a bit and worked to cushion our savings. We intended to stay in Sonoma County temporarily until we could get things sorted out, and figure out a future direction and plan of action. We didn't know it yet then, but we were home—accidentally. I write this now, still in Sonoma County, twenty-seven years later.

AFTER THE MAST

We eventually bought a fixer-upper home. At first, our idea was to refurbish Cowabunga to prepare her for a future trip—someday. In reality, though, the energy and money needed for both a fixer-upper boat and house proved too much, and we had to make a choice.

We donated *Cowabunga* to a good home, and one warm fall day, a large crane raised all of her sleek forty-two feet onto a large trailer. It was heart wrenching to watch her carted off with a new owner. Michel, Sean, Brendan, and I all watched in silence. Michel followed the convoy out with his car as far as the freeway on-ramp. The driver tooted a farewell honk, and then Michel let go.

Well, no. We haven't ever really "let go."

Cowabunga was our home, our life, and even our family name. It defined us, it was a chunk of our history, and still today, it is very much a part of who we are. After all these years, I still have tears and a knot in my throat when I remember the day she was trucked away from us. I don't think I even quite understand the emotional attachment we all had for what was really our soulmate.

The word "boat" seems so impersonal. *Cowabunga* was not an inanimate object. We learned so much about places in the world, cultures, ourselves, survival, tragedy, and joy through that vessel.

In the years that followed, while the boys were growing up, Michel and I pursued our careers as best we could, albeit a little late in the game. Contrary to our original blueprints, I didn't become a star foreign correspondent for *Time* Magazine as I had dreamed, and Michel didn't become architecture's next Frank Lloyd Wright. But because we never hesitated to embrace an exploit or wander down the path less trodden, we managed to have some interesting career and life twists. I like to believe *Cowabunga* helped give us the can-do attitudes that benefited our lives on land.

Within just a year of our residency in California, Michel found himself as the interim County Architect for Solano County. In another twist of fate, he became involved in an engineering project for the 1996 Olympic Games in Atlanta, Georgia. I stayed more local, working as a newspaper reporter, which later evolved into writing and editing for clients. Since our thirst for adventure has not been quenched, we continue to seek solace in exploring other shores, such as Fiji, Chile, Vietnam. I even spent thirty-five days walking 500 miles of the fabled Spanish Camino de Santiago.

Our boys finished out their childhoods in California. While in high school, they formed a sailing team together, competing internationally and nationally in a class of high-speed sailing skiff known as a 49er. They crisscrossed the United States and Europe with their boat in tow, sailing in competitions.

Friends sometimes ask why neither Sean nor Brendan aspired to be an architect in the footsteps of their father. My response has always been that they never really saw their father in that capacity. To them, he was a sailor. That's all they knew in their formative years.

As a young man, Sean claimed he would make a career of being a professional sailor, and that being on an America's Cup team was one of his goals. He fulfilled that dream as the bowman on the French team Areva in the 2007 America's Cup in Valencia, Spain. Today, in his late-30s, Sean continues this career and is one of the few premier elite professional sailors on the worldwide racing circuit.

Brendan's love for the outdoors manifests as a passion for rock climbing. He is always seeking to conquer the new challenges of a cliff or sheer rock face. Thriving on adrenaline and vanquishing the impossible are a part of who he is, and Brendan includes his outdoor passion with his professional career as a paramedic with a busy Denver, Colorado fire department. He, his wife, and two small children grab every available moment to pile into their custom-designed camping van, and hit the trails across the country—and even abroad.

They are adventurous, nature-driven young men. It's in their blood. With what I call the "Spirit of Cowabunga," both Sean and Brendan continue to live adventurous, non-conventional lives and are earnestly passing on the Spirit of Cowbunga to their own children. We are proud of them all.

While I do have regrets of not having continued on to other shores with *Cowabunga*, I don't regret our life on land, nor our adventures and misadventures that led us here. Yes, some of our misfortunes were self-inflicted and due to bad decisions. We acknowledge that. However, we chose a certain life with *Cowabunga*, and all four of us grew, learned, and changed with the experience. There were some amazing moments, and while not always easy, both Michel and I can honestly say we have no regrets. Even in our darkest moments, we always seemed to fall right back on our feet again. It was our school of life.

Today, Michel and I have been married for over forty years. While we don't have the perfect marriage, we have a profound relationship and the love and knowledge for each other that we can stick it out and move on to the next chapter. *Cowabunga* is our history, and her mementos are sprinkled throughout our home, just like my beloved kitchen tongs. Michel and I remember pieces of our incredible journey each day, and through those memories, the spirit and legacy of *Cowabunga* live on.

GLOSSARY

Aft- At or near the back end of a boat.

Anchorage- The part of the harbor where boats and ships are allowed to anchor (not to be mistaken for Anchorage- the most populated city in Alaska, located in the Cook Inlet, on the Southern shore of the state).

Anti-fouling paint- A marine-specific toxic paint that discourages barnacles and marine growth from clinging to the hull.

Automatic Wind Vane Pilot- An independent self-steering device. Although not "automatic" in a battery-powered sense, it allows the boat to sail autonomously thanks to a wind vane sensor connected to the boat's steering mechanism with cables or ropes, synchronizing it with the rudder.

Barograph- A device used to measure atmospheric pressure to analyze the weather. It then records the readings on a moving chart.

Becalmed- When a boat is motionless or at a standstill due to lack of wind.

Bilge- The lowest inner part of a boat's hull.

Boom- A horizontal pole, or spar, attached at a right angle to a mast, to which the bottom of a sail is attached.

Bow- The front end of a boat.

CARE- A humanitarian organization. For more information, visit www.care.org

Channel Buoy- A floating navigation signal that makes a safe passageway through a channel or waterway.

Charter Captain- The commander of a private ship that has been reserved for use.

Cockpit- The space where the captain of the boat maneuvers the craft, including the seat and instruments.

Companionway- A set of steps from the boat's deck to the cabin or deck below.

Compass Heading- The direction a boat is heading, based on using a compass and the degrees from True North.

Cowabunga- The 42-foot sailboat the owners used for sailing around the world for 10 years.

Currents- Channels of flowing water in the ocean that are strong and quick-changing.

Depth Sounder- A navigation instrument that uses sonar to determine the depth of the water.

Dinghy- A small boat, with an outboard motor, that is stored on the deck of the sailboat, for easy access to the shore.

Draft- Another name for a keel; a large weighted, fin-like structure underneath the boat, which stabilizes it and keeps it in balance, avoiding a capsize.

Du Jour- Feature of the day, as in "soup du jour," or "special of the day."

Expats- Short for "expatriates," a person who lives outside of their own native country.

Fjords- A long, narrow inlet with steep sides.

Forestay Cable- The main cable that leads from the top of the mast down to the front end of the boat.

Fromage Blanc- A type of thick creamy white French cheese, similar to sour cream or a thick yogurt consistency.

Front Roller Furling Sail- A sail specially designed to be rolled, or reefed, (usually the front sail, headsail, jib, or genoa), around a rotating stay (headstay or forestay), or the front rigging, in order to reduce in size to be manageable under strong or varying wind conditions.

Galley- A small kitchen or cooking area on a boat.

General Delivery- A service where mail can be delivered to a post office and the addressee can pick it up from there (as of 2017, this service may be limited or unavailable; check local regulations before attempting).

Genoa Sail- The front sail on a sailboat.

Halyards- The ropes or cables used to hoist the sails along or toward the mast.

Harbormaster- The person officially in charge of operations in a harbor.

Headpiece Attachment- A heavy duty rectangular stainless-steel piece, or plate, that bolts the roller furling system and headstay to the top of the mast.

Headstay- On a sailboat, it's a rope or wire support from the mast to the bow.

Heavy Tubes- The metal alloy roller furling tubes that enclose the headstay or forestay, with a full-length groove along which the genoa sail was housed.

Horizon- The apparent line where the sky meets the earth or ocean.

Hull- The bottommost part of a boat or ship that is mostly submerged underwater.

Jerrycans- A flat-sided can used to store or transport liquids, usually around 4-5 gallons in size.

Jetty- A pier or rock structure that projects into a body of water to protect the harbor from storms and erosion.

Jib– A type of headsail on a sailboat.

Jury-rig- To make a temporary or makeshift piece of equipment.

Keel- A large weighted, fin-like structure underneath the boat, which stabilizes and keeps the boat in balance, avoiding a capsize.

Ketch- A two-masted sailboat with a smaller mast (or the mizzen) in the rear or back end of the boat.

Lagoon- A smaller, shallow body of water off from the ocean by a reef or sandbar.

Lagoon- The local name given to a specific protected anchorage in Dakar where other cruising yachts were anchored.

Lawrence of Arabia- A reference to the legendary hero who led the Arabians in a battle against Turkey.

Lee Cloth- A canvas for the open side of that bunk that hooks from under the mattress and attaches to the ceiling so the occupant can't fall out, especially with the boat in motion.

Lion's Club- An International organization dedicated to community service and good international relations.

Log- An official, written record of events and observations on a boat.

Log Book- A book where the official, written record of events and observations on a boat are maintained.

Mainsail- The principal sail on a boat, held triangularly by the main mast and bordered by the boom along the bottom of the sail.

Marina- An area of water with docks for storing boats and offering other boating services.

Marine Charts and Tables- The written records where navigational data would be plotted on a regular basis to estimate boat's position; also pre-printed maps and mathematical calculations used to assist in plotting positions.

Masts- Pole-like structures above the hull and upper portions of a boat to hold sails, spars, rigging, booms, signals.

Medina- An ancient, native part of a North African city.

Mizzen Boom- Horizontal pole, or spar, attached at a right angle to the mizzen mast, or the aft mast located towards the back of the boat, to which the bottom of the mizzen sail is attached.

Mizzen Mast- The mast of a smaller stabilizing sail, similar in shape to the main mast, but at the rear of the boat.

Naval Signal Flags- Fabric flags that are used to communicate with other ships through an international code.

Navigable- Passable; a body of water where a boat can safely sail.

NGO- "Non-government Organization," a non-profit organization independent of the government.

Paseo- Traditional evening time in Spain when families leisurely walk around and relax after their day of work.

Pilot Boats- A small boat, usually used to transport pilots to and from ships.

Pilotine- The latin translation of a pilot boat, and a term used in some foreign harbors to designate a small pilot boat.

Port- The left-hand side of a ship.

Port- A city or town located on a waterway, usually with facilities for ships.

Rias- The Spanish translation for a particular inlet similar to a fjord.

Roller Furler- The device or entire system that rolls, reefs, or furls a sail around a rotating stay (headstay or forestay), or the front rigging, in order the reduce the sail to a manageable size under strong or varying wind conditions.

Roller Furling Drum- The large round device at the bottom of the roller furling system to which the front sail (jib or genoa) is attached, allowing the sail to roll around on itself as the head-stay or forestay turns, reducing the size of the sail.

Sextant- A navigation instrument that measures the angle between the sun and the horizon in relation to a boat's position on the sea to assist in plotting the boat's latitude and longitude.

Sextant Sun Sights- The measurements taken with the sun using a sextant to determine one's geographical position at sea.

Sheets- The ropes attached at the bottom ends of the sails that wrap around winches to hold the sails tight to the deck in the best position for that specific wind angle.

Spinnaker- A front sail used for sailing downwind.

Stanchions- The upright deck perimeter stainless steel support poles.

Starboard- The right-hand side of a ship.

Stern- The back part of a boat.

Tack- A pattern of zig-zagging in order to sail into the wind.

The High Seas- The open waters of the ocean, usually three or more miles from shore.

Tidal Wave- A large wave in a body of water, sometimes caused by an earthquake.

Tipo- The Portuguese translation of the word "Type (of)."

Trawler- A kind of fishing boat.

Turnbuckle- A vital tension-adjusting device for the rigging on the stays.

VHF Radio- "Very High Frequency," a type of radio used to communicate at sea.

Visa- A document that allows temporary entry into another country.

Wharf- A structure of the shore of a harbor, where ships can dock, they often include warehouses, piers and other facilities.

Winch Handle- The handle on the device used to wind or unwind a rope or cable.

Winches- A mechanical device used to wind up or unwind a rope or cable.

Yachtie- Sailors traveling and living long term on their boats, also referred to as "cruisers."

FIRST APPEARANCES

The basis of the book began as 44 vignettes that first appeared on the author's website, <www.janiscouvreux.com> Although significantly changed and edited to best fit a book format, they originally fell under the title "Blog from the Past," later becoming "Vignettes from Cowabunga." Additionally, several pieces from this book originated from published works. Though changed from their original context, we would like to extend credit and appreciation to all publications who first gave the story of Cowabunga a readership:

"Thirty Days: I Sailed Across the Ocean with Two Children," July 30, 2015,
Luna y Luna Magazine, now *Luna Luna Magazine*: <www.lunalunamagazine.com>

Longreads picked up the same vignette, reprinting Luna Luna's publication on July 31, 2015 with credit going to Luna Luna:
<https://longreads.com/2015/07/31/sailing-across-the-atlantic-in-30-days-with-two-toddlers/>

"We Sailed Across the Ocean in 30 Days with 2 Children—And Lived to Tell About It," November 11, 2015, *Huffington Post;* with first printing credit given to Luna Luna Magazine. Janis was subsequently invited to blog for them.

Several of her other Huffington Post blog posts are variation of a theme of the Couvreux's sailing life, and can be viewed at :<http://www.huffingtonpost.com/author/janis-couvreux>

"The Spring that Sprung (Why My Broken Kitchen Tongs Brought Me to Tears)," September 2015, *Foliate Oak Literary Magazine*: <http://janiscouvreux.com/in-the-news/foliate-oak-magazine-features-story-that-sprung/>, or on their website: <http://www.foliateoak.com/janis-lasky-couvreux.html>

"Stranger in the Night," which is now part of the chapter on Fortaleza, was the first place Adult Nonfiction winner at the February 2017 San Francisco Writers Conference, <https://sfwriters.org/contest-winners> winning under the title "Sail Cowabunga! A Family's Ten Years at Sea."

Most recently Janis has blogged for *Pryme Magazine*, <http://prymemag.com/author/janiscouvreux/> and *The Lady Alliance*, <http://www.theladyalliance.com/janis-articles> These are entirely new posts that are not takes on or edited versions of her vignettes.

Acknowledgements

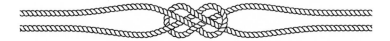

Before I could write this story, I had to live it: the before, during, and after. The "after" part took the longest. It needed to age, be digested, and gain perspective. As my grandchildren began to arrive upon the scene, I knew I had to record this for them so they could better understand their fathers and the path that brought them here. They are still too young to read and understand it, and that may only come after Michel and I are gone, but this story will be tucked away somewhere in their lives.

One doesn't live a life all by oneself, and our path crossed a lifetime of people across four continents. There were so many players and life-savers in our adventure along the way that I can't list them all here. Some we have never seen again, some we occasionally reconnect with, and some have become dear friends. Know that we cherish you all in our hearts and memories for the crucial parts you played in our lives. However, I would like to give particular mention to the Guapo (Schürmann) family, the Martin family, the Schaefer family, the Jakaranda (Bungener) family, and the Pradin family. Thanks to Gregory Jaynes, a former journalist at Time and Life magazines, who featured us in two articles and was an immense inspiration to me; and to the many friends, neighbors, and colleagues from the past and present who encouraged me over the years to write this story.

To my husband, Michel: without him and his love I would never have lived such an adventure, nor learned from the misadventures, and thanks to his nudging, I finally wrote it all down.

I had the luxury of writing this book over several years through brief installments, as my inspiration would wax and wane. Michel often wondered if anything would come of it, but I knew how my writer's brain worked, and I couldn't rush. The story was still aging. I am eternally grateful to my first editor Elaine Silver who flushed out my original manuscript flaws, and to Myra Fiacco of Filles Vertes Publishing for her vision, enthusiasm, and love for this story. Myra and I were assisted by the remarkable team she assembled to polish and mold this chronicle. I extend my sincere gratitude to editors Mary Terra Berns for her frank questions, precise comments, and additional fine tuning; Kaylynn Hills for weeding out more unnecessary fluff and ill-placed tenses; and Melissa Thiringer for one final encompassing round. Myra took special care and attention to keep me in every loop and facet of the production of this book. Particular mention goes to Myra and Kate Cowan of Broken Arrow Designs for their vision of a cover design and their inclusion of Michel and me in the process so that everyone involved would be pleased with the result.

In memoriam for Philippe Larrue and Pierre Binot, this book has a special place of indebtedness in Michel's heart for these two friends' part in our adventure.

ABOUT THE AUTHOR

Janis Lasky Couvreux is an award-winning writer, journalist, Franco-American, lover of languages, travel and adventure addict, sailor, mom, and grandmom. Formerly a newspaper reporter and freelance journalist, Janis is currently a blogger at *Huffington Post*, *Pryme Magazine*, and *The Lady Alliance*, where she writes about living bilingually, crossing oceans, backpacking adventures, and raising kids outside the box. Some of Janis' vignettes have been recently published in *Luna Luna Magazine*, *Longreads*, and *Foliate Oak Literary Magazine*, and she won the first place Adult Nonfiction award at the 2017 San Francisco Writers Conference.

EXPLORE MORE TITLES BY
FILLES VERTES PUBLISHING

FILLES VERTES
PUBLISHING

Visit us at

www.fillesvertespublishing.com/shop

to view our other titles and enjoy 20% off with the coupon code

"MoreFVP"